EMERGING MARKETS

OTHER ECONOMIST BOOKS

Guide to Analysing Companies
Guide to Business Modelling
Guide to Business Planning
Guide to Economic Indicators
Guide to the European Union
Guide to Financial Markets
Guide to Management Ideas
Numbers Guide
Style Guide

Dictionary of Business
Dictionary of Economics
International Dictionary of Finance

Brands and Branding
Business Ethics
Business Strategy
China's Stockmarket
E-trends
Globalisation
Successful Innovation
Successful Mergers
Wall Street

Essential Director
Essential Economics
Essential Finance
Essential Internet
Essential Investment
Essential Negotiation

Pocket Asia
Pocket Europe in Figures
Pocket World in Figures

EMERGING MARKETS

Lessons for business success and
the outlook for different markets

Nenad Pacek

and

Daniel Thorniley

THE ECONOMIST IN ASSOCIATION WITH
PROFILE BOOKS LTD

Published by Profile Books Ltd
3A Exmouth House, Pine Street, London EC1R 0JH
www.profilebooks.com

Typeset in EcoType by MacGuru Ltd
info@macguru.org.uk

Printed and bound in Great Britain by
Creative Print and Design (Wales), Ebbw Vale

A CIP catalogue record for this book is available
from the British Library

ISBN-10: 1 86197 408 6
ISBN-13: 978 1 86197 408 2

Contents

THIS BOOK IS DEDICATED TO

my wife, Antonia, and daughter, Nina,
and to my parents and sister (NP)

my wife, Maria, and daughter, Natasha, and to my parents,
Harry and Irene, and brother, Paul (DT)

Preface

Just look at these newspaper headlines: "L'Oréal Says Net Climbed 20% on Strong Emerging Markets"; or "Emerging Markets Enable Nestlé to Lift Earnings 13%"; or "Chinese Growth Helps to Lift Coke Earnings". A glance behind the scenes reveals that L'Oréal's growth in China, for example, has more than tripled since 1997, its Russian business is growing more than 50% per year and its sales in most other leading emerging markets are growing well over 20% a year.

There is no doubt that emerging markets offer enormous opportunities to companies with strong growth ambitions. But although some companies perform well in emerging markets, many that are equally ambitious end up frustrated and far from reaching their initial targets.

The aim of this book is to help businesses avoid the mistakes many multinationals have made in emerging markets. It covers everything that businesses need to think about, understand and act on in order to be successful in emerging markets. Real corporate experiences are used wherever possible to illustrate the points made and we are grateful and indebted to the many executives who over the years have shared with us their lessons of business success and failure in emerging markets. There are many references to conversations with and remarks made by them, but as a professional courtesy and because it makes no difference to the points we illustrate, we have chosen not to give names even when conversations were on the record. Where names do appear, the remarks and quotations were not made to the authors personally and are in the public domain.

We are grateful to our former colleague and friend, Jeremy Kourdi, who encouraged us to write the book; to Delia Meth-Cohn, who helped edit the book, provided additional examples and advised on the book's structure; to colleagues in The Economist Corporate Network, Asia, for insights into business in South-East Asia; and to Stephen Brough, Penny Williams and Martin Liu for the parts they have played in the book's creation.

We are also keen to hear from anyone who would like to share their experiences of emerging markets or would like to know more about The Economist Corporate Network. You can email us on nenadpacek @economist.com and danielthorniley@economist.com.

Nenad Pacek and Daniel Thorniley, March 2004

1
LESSONS FOR BUSINESS SUCCESS

1 Why companies fail

If I want sustainable profits, I am going to invest in the longer term, even if it has a negative impact on the short term. For some of the members of the financial community, whose timeframe is between half a year and a year, it is very difficult to explain what it means to build up a business in Korea or China or Russia, where you have to invest for five to ten years before you get into profitability.

Peter Brabeck, CEO of Nestlé, who refuses to give short-term financial targets to analysts. Nestlé has had a total annual shareholder return of 16.8% over a ten-year period and emerging markets account for 25% of its total global sales.

It does not matter how much it costs. What matters is how much money it can make.

Roberto Goizueta, former CEO of Coca-Cola. (Coca-Cola is still the most valuable brand in the world. Since December 2002 it has refused to give quarterly and annual sales expectations to analysts.)

Market leaders in their sector in the developed world often set out to repeat their success in emerging markets, and seemingly put a lot of resources into achieving their aim. This chapter looks at the reasons so many fail – and what can be done to make sure they do not.

Growth is a corporate obsession. For many companies, one of the best ways to achieve steady organic growth is through steady geographical expansion. Coca-Cola's share price jumped 3,500% between 1981 and 1997, for example, as the company almost quintupled in size, mostly thanks to bold investments in emerging markets. But time and time again firms that are market leaders in the developed world fail to replicate that success in emerging markets. Why? And what can companies do about it?

The problem typically starts at the top of the corporate hierarchy. A typical scenario goes like this. A CEO sends a manager that he knows and trusts to start "conquering" a group of countries in the developing world. This manager ends up operating from a regional hub. He visits the countries he is interested in, establishes contacts and collects relevant information. He spends months evaluating potential distributors and partners. He decides who he wants to work with and signs the contracts. Sales begin. He hires a few people in the hub to co-ordinate the effort. Sales pick up. He is excited. Business is going well. "We are in. The sky is the limit", or so he thinks.

A year later he is holding a report on market shares. "How can this small player be ahead? Why am I still so far behind?" His CEO calls and says: "I'm looking at the report. It is not bad. But I would like to see us becoming much more dominant next year."

Another year on, the position is much the same. Business is slightly up but not relative to the competition. This time the CEO is less relaxed: "You said you were going to increase our market share. What's wrong?" This is when the regional manager usually says: "I think I'll need more resources to build the business. People don't seem to know our brands here."

The CEO's response is: "Prove to me there is more business there and you'll get more resources." To which the inevitable riposte is: "How can I increase sales if you don't allow me to invest more?"

Getting out of this vicious circle is never easy. The following guidelines show how a firm can avoid getting into it and improve its chances of being successful in an emerging market.

Ensure there is genuine commitment from the very top

Senior management must be absolutely committed to an emerging-market business. It must commit sufficient resources to getting it established and then to sustaining and growing it. Building business in emerging markets is never a short-term affair; the CEO and the board must be prepared to lose money for a number of years. In companies that prove successful in emerging markets, it is common that once a strategic commitment has been made, the CEO appoints a trusted senior manager who is powerful enough to override internal obstacles and to make investment decisions according to market needs. He champions and drives the emerging-market business. CEOs of companies that are successful in emerging markets have often made a point of convincing analysts and shareholders about the benefits of the long-term growth that emerging markets can help provide. Companies that focus on short-term profit maximisation are typically less successful in emerging markets, even if their products dominate the developed world.

Never take market leadership for granted

Just because a company is a market leader in the developed world, it does not mean that it will become a market leader in an emerging market. Consumers in emerging markets are often unaware of a newly available product or of its brand recognition in the developed world. Companies that are early into the market and put resources into skilful brand building and local presence usually end up dominating the market, even if they are small, local players. Multinationals that underestimate the potential competition from smaller international and domestic competitors do so at their peril.

Toe-dipping often backfires

Either go for it or stay out. Half-baked entry and market testing is dangerous. John Menzer, who took over Wal-Mart's international operations in 1999, told the *Financial Times* in early 2003:

> No more flag-planting and opening a few stores to test out the market. Now when we decide to go into a new market, we are going to go in with enough mass that we can use our core competences.

Wal-Mart learned some bitter lessons in several markets in Latin America where it was beaten by smaller European competitors. While the US giant was testing the market, Europeans were developing it at full speed and now enjoy the benefits of that approach.

Don't let economic crises interfere with strategy: adjust performance criteria

A Dow Chemical regional executive for Europe, Middle East and Africa says:

> Our company accepts that there are regular setbacks and crises in emerging markets. We know that most of these crises are largely crises of progress and we do not really adjust our overall strategic approach. We adjust our tactics but we are never really concerned about crises. They come and go and we are here to stay.

Economic and political uncertainties can easily disrupt quarterly and even annual plans. This goes with the territory and many companies do not even adjust their cost structure in times of downturn, knowing that this can damage the business once the crisis is over. The wisdom of this approach was demonstrated after the 1998 rouble crisis in Russia. In a *Wall Street Journal* interview in 2002, Peter Brabeck, CEO of Nestlé, said:

*If I had only thought about short-term profit margins, I would
have withdrawn from Russia, like everybody else, during the
Russian crisis. We did not. It very clearly had an impact on my
profit margins, but in 18 months we doubled our market share.
This is the difference between short-term profit margin
maximisation and long-term, sustainable profitable growth.*

It is immensely frustrating for regional managers to be criticised for
missing quarterly budgets during crises. Performance criteria should be
focused on sustainable, medium- to long-term results, not the next
month or quarter. Likewise, management incentive schemes should be
related to longer-term results.

Be early to market and go for it

As emerging markets mature, it becomes harder to persuade consumers
to switch brands and take market share from established products, as it
is in the developed world where firms celebrate if they manage to
increase their market shares by 0.5% in a year. What surprises many
companies is how quickly a competitive business environment can
develop in emerging markets, despite their relative lack of economic
sophistication and occasional crises. Companies that allow other players to dominate the market for too long (through a half-hearted
approach or by late entry or both) always find it difficult to turn things
around. While mighty Wrigley dithered about expanding into Russia,
for example, Dandy, a small privately held Danish company, captured
almost the entire local market. It took Wrigley years and millions of dollars to catch up.

Be flexible

Unwillingness to change long-standing practices is probably one of the
largest obstacles to success in emerging markets. Different markets
require a temporary or even lasting departure from the ways in which a
company is used to operating. Rather than saying "We don't do this anywhere in the world", several carmakers gave up their long struggle to
find local partners and extended their operations to include sales and
distribution of their products. This flexibility was driven by the realisation that they would not succeed without fully committed partners. By
taking control, they were able to establish lasting and sustainable
market leadership quickly. Such flexibility does not have to be costly; it
just has to be creative. When Ford could not find a distributor in

Bulgaria it asked its German distributor to do the job. Two years later (while competing carmakers were still searching for good local partners), Ford had a dominant market lead.

Adapt to the market

Customers are often more price-sensitive in emerging markets, but many companies stick to their product portfolio and pricing structures instead of adapting their products and marketing to take local sensitivities into account. As a result, their market share remains small compared with lower-priced competitors offering products that local consumers or businesses prefer to buy.

Localise decision-making and empower regional and country managers

One of IBM's regional bosses for Central Eastern Europe, Middle East and Africa (CEEMEA) says he constantly has difficulties moving corporate decision-making forward. Senior management is slow to allow local managers to step up business development. He comments:

> We should just let our country managers run the show as they
> see fit based on local circumstances. We as a centre can
> provide guidance, all kinds of support and teach them lessons
> of success and failure from other markets.

It is clear that companies that give more decision-making power to their local managers – particularly in marketing, sales, pay and bonuses – usually do better than the centralisers. However, companies that leave all the decision-making to their local partners are often just saving on costs. It is local underinvestment that explains what distinguishes losers from winners.

Underinvestment is often a result of focusing on short-term rather than longer-term results, especially in listed companies. Roberto Goizueta, former CEO of Coca-Cola, who championed investments in emerging markets, was famous for taking issue with analysts when they criticised the company for its quarterly earnings and "reckless investments". He also made his regional managers accountable for three-year results (not one quarter or one year). When Goizueta took over as CEO, he was stunned to discover how little say the company had about how its product was marketed around the world because of its reliance on partners to look after such things.

7

Pay attention to organisational structure – and even more to processes

Many companies discuss at length what kind of organisational structure they should employ in emerging markets. They focus on location of offices, reporting lines and where certain business functions should be located. These are all relevant considerations – and for more on corporate structures see Chapter 7.

But what many companies (even those who understand the importance of having an excellent local presence) ignore are the organisational processes. Local managers should be made accountable for results but given considerable freedom of action. Goizueta had the following message for Coca-Cola's regional and local managers:

> I want you to tell me what you need to do to expand your business, what kind of capital you need to do so, and what kind of net return you're going to get.

Another good example is GlaxoWellcome (now GlaxoSmithKline), which allowed its local managers to decide what was the best way to spend investment money, as long as they met agreed returns on investment and stuck to broad corporate guidelines. Once headquarters started to get more involved, the performance suffered.

Recognise that a worldly business requires worldly people

The senior managers who are making the overall decisions about emerging-market investments must feel comfortable in these places. They need to have a sufficiently international perspective, to have travelled and had experience of operating internationally. The closer to the market a manager is operating, the more important it is that he has a good understanding of the local market, culture and language. It is still fairly common for a company's emerging-markets business to be run by people who had never even been outside the developed world before their appointment to run an emerging-market business. Such people start with a handicap that is not easy to overcome.

Don't ignore small markets – they can offer rich opportunities

A regional boss at Oracle says:

> A $10m contract from the government of Albania is the same as a $10m contract from the government of China. We don't

*want to let our competitors get that kind of money. At Oracle
we say that no market is small, because our competition is there.*

The lack of competition in many small markets means that early
entrants and companies focusing on building a strong local presence
often earn fantastic returns on investment. In the poorest countries of
Sub-Saharan Africa, for example, one mobile telecoms company has
made a return on investment that is six times the level it achieved in
richer South Africa.

Know what you are getting into

Few companies have the resources to develop all markets at the same
time. So a company needs up-to-date knowledge of external conditions
to decide and plan the geographical order in which it should expand its
operations. Such knowledge takes time and money to acquire, but in
emerging markets there is also the difficulty that reliable data are often
hard to find. As a result, instinct or gut feeling plays an important part in
decisions to expand into developing countries. Companies can become
more comfortable with such decision-making by, for example, building
relationships and networks with people already operating in the markets in question. This is a great help in testing assumptions and in dis-
covering the realities of a market.

Know or anticipate what others are getting into

When companies prioritise the markets they are considering entering,
they often do so on the basis of a few key economic indicators. This pro-
duces hotspots, with many players pouring into some markets and few
into others. For example, as a regional star, Hungary attracted all the
major players in the mid-1990s, creating one of the tightest, most competitive markets in Europe where many firms struggled to make any
money. However, companies which anticipated how crowded the Hungarian market was going to become and opted to invest more in Russia
found themselves in a market that offered less competition, higher margins, quicker profits and more scope to build market share and brand
loyalties.

Assess and address the internal constraints

It is essential to work out what resources the company does not have
but will need to carry out its emerging market strategy. These may be
financial, product-related or human.

Set high standards and benchmark against the best

Successful companies frequently ask themselves what ideal they are aiming at in emerging markets. They set criteria and then see what they can learn from the companies that are best for each criterion.

Understand that business in emerging markets is more time-consuming

Everything takes longer than in the developed world. Dealing with local authorities, customs clearing or getting a simple licence can take days or weeks. Since time is money, companies should understand the pace at which it is possible to run the business and budget money and time accordingly.

Don't ignore emerging markets because you think they are too small

With low economic growth and increasing pressure (for most businesses) on profit margins in the developed world, emerging markets can offer higher margins and higher growth.

Never take your eye off the ball

It is really all about being thorough, and these guidelines are a good start. Companies that are not constantly alert risk failure and damage to their brands. If Mercedes had waited for its distributor to build a service facility in Moscow instead of taking control and building a facility itself, it might have taken years to recover from the brand damage the company would have suffered. (See Chapter 8 for more on reaching the local market and distribution issues.)

2 Managing corporate expectations

I never attempt to make money on the stockmarket. I buy on the assumption
that they could close the market the next day and not reopen it for five years.

Warren Buffett

The fish rots from the head.

Old Chinese saying

Business in emerging markets rarely succeeds if it is subjected to the
short-term criteria that companies in the less volatile developed
world are often judged by. But many chief executives of listed companies are unwilling to adopt longer-term targets. Managing the expectations of senior management is one of the top three critical issues for
developing a healthy business in emerging markets. This chapter
explores strategies to overcome in-built short-term perspectives and to
manage the expectations of not only board members but also investment analysts and the media, whose perceptions of a company are crucial in determining its reputation and share price.

If you look at how companies have gone about building and sustaining their business in emerging markets, two facts invariably
emerge. A short-termist approach succeeds only in the short term.
Private companies, or those not dependent on equity markets,
almost always build stronger and more sustainable businesses than
listed companies.

A short-term approach to building business in emerging markets is
the most frequent cause of longer-term failure. When companies fall
behind their more systematic competition, regional and country managers often criticise their CEOs for not releasing enough resources to
build the business properly. Many privately accuse their CEOs of caring
only about the next set of quarterly results.

That CEOs take a short-term approach is not surprising for two reasons. First, reward systems have increasingly favoured those who max-
imise short-term profits. Second, the complexity and pressure of running
large corporations have steadily decreased the shelf-life of the average
CEO. Consultants at Booz Allen Hamilton reckon that the average tenure
of CEOs for the world's 2,500 most valuable companies had fallen to
7.3 years in 2001, compared with 9.5 years in 1995. And markets give an

average CEO less than 19 months to increase the share price, according to Burson-Marsteller, a public relations company.

To the detriment of the long-term well-being of their corporations, a number of CEOs have come to see their job as maximising short-term profits while in charge. This growing short-termism in the past two decades is one of the reasons that only 40% of *Fortune* 500 companies in 1980 are still on the list today. The stockmarket madness of the late 1990s, where many tried to inflate profits via creative accounting practices, is just an extreme symptom of the same disease.

In the past two decades compensation systems for CEOs have largely been based on stock options and bonuses based on short-term profit maximisation. Rewards go to those who move the stock price up in the short term. Many CEOs choose not to miss a large annual bonus or a mega stock-option deal by investing in something that will bring returns 3–5 years later. In such companies, emerging-market business suffers the most. Success in emerging markets requires a passion for systematically building business and investments that will not bring in profits next quarter or even in the next three years. Unfortunately, investing for the medium to longer term has increasingly been viewed as a cost that squeezes the all-important short-term profits.

Short-termism reached its peak during the stockmarket bubble of the late 1990s. Many CEOs of listed companies, particularly in the United States and the UK, were under pressure to provide high short-term returns to their increasingly impatient shareholders. Managers operating in emerging markets found themselves (and many still do) impossibly pressured by the contradictions in overall policy. On the one hand they were being told to increase growth (and short-term returns); on the other hand they were being refused the resources to systematically build up business.

Many well-run companies' stock prices were (and continue to be) severely punished for missing expected quarterly earnings by an unforgiving Wall Street, as if such results really mattered for the overall soundness and future prospects of the business. Good decisions aimed at building a sustainable business are rarely rewarded by the herd-like behaviour of large institutional investors. Although this attitude has started to change following the bursting of the stockmarket bubble, short-termism among investors, and subsequently CEOs, remains alive and kicking. Fund managers and analysts are frequently rewarded on how well they do in one quarter and how well they predict quarterly earnings. This contributes to the steadily growing and damaging phenomenon of herd behaviour. "I buy because others do. I sell when I see that others sell," is how one youngish fund manager described how he worked.

Read the transcripts of CEOs' conference calls with stock analysts and it is clear that business decisions relating to the future development of publicly listed companies are largely irrelevant. A recent study reported in the *Harvard Business Review* in June 2001, done by doctoral candidates at New York University's Stern School of Business, found that more than 90% of analysts' questions to CEOs during conference calls were about expectations for the next quarter's earnings. Investments were treated as factors that might jeopardise this "holy" quarterly number. Analysts' behaviour is unlikely to change. They cover many companies, and according to one analyst: "There is really no time to properly research, analyse and think."

No wonder the managers who are in charge of real business decisions are immensely irritated by analysts. A senior executive from one of the 100 largest corporations in the world (and a rare highly successful company in emerging markets) said in a private conversation:

> These 26-year-olds, who have never run any business, come to us and interrogate us like the Gestapo. They are not interested in how we build business or what we are trying to do. And the day after they reveal our plans on CNBC, another damaging influence by the way. Because we told them about our investments our share price went down 15% in a few hours. We should do what XYZ does – give them a vague idea what the plans are and tell them to go to hell.

The impact of all this on business is clear. Many companies have postponed relevant or even crucial investments for their future, and some will have trouble surviving as years go by. One regional executive says:

> We make an enormous number of business decisions that I would never do if I were a sole owner of this business. But our top management is more obsessed with the steady growth of quarterly earnings than investing for the future. We will soon run into severe problems.

Short-termism is problematic for sound business decision-making in general. But for decision-making in emerging markets it is disastrous.

Many companies invest too little in preparing for market entry (relative to the best competition) or have inadequate resources to execute sound market entry and market expansion plans (see later chapters).

So how do emerging-market managers go about managing the expectations of senior management? First they should go through the checklist in Chapter 3 and fight to get the resources to prepare each aspect of market entry properly. Without thorough preparation, any manager will have a hard time growing an emerging-market business, and the task of managing the CEO's expectations will become monumental.

Emerging markets are often more volatile than developed markets. There are years that are spectacularly good but they usually do not last. How can emerging-market managers predict the sustainable annual growth of business over, say, the next five years? How do they explain the inevitable ups and downs, and how do they get senior management to accept that next year may not be as good as the previous one?

There is a tendency for CEOs to say: "Your business jumped 55% last year. You can do better than that or at least as well." Emerging-market managers need to communicate constantly what is shaping their business, taking care to point out why a certain level of performance may not be sustainable and the factors and risks which might set things back. Equally, senior management needs to be made aware that there are years when sales fall to unexpectedly low levels, usually because of some kind of emerging-market crisis (see Chapter 14). As with good years, the circumstances that made a year a bad one usually do not last. Markets bounce back sooner or later. Many short-termist companies react to such crises by radically downsizing operations. Although this provides short-term protection, it may have negative implications in the longer term (see Chapter 14).

Many CEOs push regional managers to work to stretched budgets, which simply increases the stress of working in a volatile and difficult to predict market. Or it is counterproductive because managers simply ignore the budget as it does not take into account the realities of the market. The message from the top is often: "You claim there is a lot of potential in emerging markets, let's see it." And that is regardless of the fact that the risk and uncertainty as well as the potential have been pointed out.

One problem is that many companies push managers to deliver big returns before enough has been invested in establishing local market presence and securing brand recognition. But even in companies that do invest in what they need to, budget games are rampant. Those who meet and beat budgetary targets (regardless of how low they were set) are usu-ally regarded as better managers than those who grow a business faster year on year but keep missing their unrealistic budgetary targets.

Many potentially productive hours of work are wasted on tactics for meeting budgetary expectations. As the regional manager of a large American company says: "I spend too much time managing the bottom line instead of managing the business." Studies by Wharton business school show that setting what managers perceive as overly ambitious goals distorts their behaviour and ultimately damages their companies. Managers start playing games. If they see they can exceed the stretch budget, for example, they try and delay end-of-year sales so they are booked in the next year. They fear that fantastic growth will earn them an even worse budgetary target next year, and they also want to have a good start to the year. Some managers even give up hard work "to prove that the target was crazy" and to play down expectations for the next year. As one manager who lost his job after proving that the target was crazy said: "I lost my job but at least I'll stay sane." The volatility of emerging markets makes the requirement to meet demanding budgets particularly stressful for local and regional managers, with the result that they are even more likely to behave in ways that are not in the best long-term interests of their firms.

Budget games are a fact of corporate life, but for emerging markets the following approach is a good one to adopt.

Determine the sustainable level of business growth in a given market

This assessment should be based on at least three factors: past results (if any); a thorough understanding of the external environment and the risks it carries; and a clear view of the internal capabilities and resources (see Chapter 3).

Decide whether you can communicate this analysis openly

Depending on the company culture and the CEO, some managers are able truthfully to communicate this sustainability analysis to their senior management. But in many companies it is not possible for at least two reasons. One is that pay and bonuses are linked to exceeding tar-gets, and furthermore, missing a target can lose you your job or damage your career.

As a result, many companies have developed a corporate culture of deceit and caution. If a manager thinks his business in an emerging market can grow 30% next year, he will tell his senior management that a sustainable rate of growth is 15% plus, while pointing out a whole set of things that can potentially destroy even this 15% growth rate.

Point out all risks to the main scenario

Clearly outlining risk factors, as a footnote to the budget and business plan, is a smart thing to do in emerging markets regardless of whether a company encourages and rewards truthful communication or is infested with a culture of deceit. In both cases, senior management needs to be aware of the things that can go wrong. There is no shortage of risks in emerging markets. Many companies active in them say that the single biggest risk affecting their emerging-market plans in the last decade was the unpredictability of currency devaluations. Managers at Sony say that they fear unpredictable recessions and unpredictable consumer behaviour. In many countries, managers worry about political risks and the way they affect sales. In years of uncertain elections, for example, consumers' appetite for spending often shrinks. Perhaps the most worrying thing for many companies is that the list of largely unpredictable market threats is long, even in reasonably well managed emerging markets. The Mexico crisis in 1994 moved the country from a star to a short-term basket case in a matter of weeks, for no good fundamental reason (see Chapter 14).

Make sure senior management understands and accepts volatility

One of the most important things for senior management to accept is that emerging markets are volatile. Regardless of how much money is invested and regardless of the quality of the people running the operation on the ground, there will be bad years and there will be good years, even spectacular ones. Also keep in mind that not all global emerging markets are down at the same time. The encouraging news is that there are, in virtually all emerging markets, more good years than bad ones. In other words, there is steady long-term growth of revenues and profits. But both good and bad years often come unexpectedly, despite the efforts of forecasters to predict the future.

Establish different performance criteria for emerging markets

Managers operating in emerging markets need to be judged according to different criteria from those operating in developed markets. Performance criteria should focus on sustainable medium- to long-term results.

Pay and rewards should be linked to these and not to short-term results. This will encourage more truthful and meaningful exchanges of information and analysis between country, regional and senior managers. It will also create a corporate culture in which emerging-market setbacks are seen as a normal part of business (and often economic progress) and not as disasters.

Educate senior management about risks and opportunities

One of the most important priorities for those in charge of emerging markets is to make senior management clearly aware of the risks and opportunities in their territory. Senior management's perceptions are inevitably shaped by news headlines, which do not tell the whole story, or even the true one. The best type of education is to bring the CEO and senior management to the market. But with such visits it is crucial to convey the realities of a market. For example, in most emerging markets there is a large difference in development and purchasing power between capital cities and the rest of the country. A CEO who gets only a picture of a booming capital and a five-star hotel might start making unreasonable demands later on. In other words, sell the market to the CEO but do not oversell it.

To provide more objectivity to the visit, bring in outside speakers. These not only provide an expert view of the market, they also bridge any gap in trust between senior management and those on the ground. If an outside expert talks about the opportunities and risks of business in the market, it adds credibility to the local management's arguments.

In a globalised world there is a growing tendency in business to believe emerging markets are less foreign, less different, than they are. Senior managers have to be made aware of these foreign differences and the differences they make to business performance. At the same time, they must not become scared of them; that will only lead to a lack of commitment to a market in terms of resources.

3 Market entry preparation

A traveller without knowledge is a bird without wings.

Sa'di Gulistan, 13th century

Many companies mess up their entry into an emerging market by not adequately preparing the ground. This chapter provides a comprehensive run-down of the issues that must be understood and acted on before market entry is attempted.

Virtually all multinational companies do most of their business and make most of their profits in the developed world, and because their emerging-market business is smaller in absolute terms (and perhaps they understand it less), senior managers often pay less attention to it. Nevertheless, many CEOs put a lot of emphasis on being a powerful global player and being strong in emerging markets. The reality is less glorious. Time and time again, companies enter new markets with little understanding of what they are getting into, and then wonder why their often smaller competitors are beating them hands down.

Thorough preparation is essential for success. Leadership and support in the form of finance and other resources must come from the top of the corporate hierarchy from the very beginning. Any half-hearted effort is eventually bound to fail in the face of international and domestic competition. Making the necessary investment in preparation is usually more expensive than is generally thought, but strangely, many companies will spend millions after they decide on a market entry or expansion plan but will not spend much trying to understand what they are getting into in the first place. Worse still, many leading firms under-invest in both preparation and execution, and later wonder what went wrong.

Business plans for emerging-market operations must be based on sound assumptions. Understanding the external environment should be a continuous effort, not just a one-off or occasional exercise. It should include extensive and continuous research. But none of this is much use if the company does not have or is not prepared to use internal resources to address the challenges of the external environment.

The external audit

The first priority is to rank markets according to the political and economic environment and the business environment. Many of the things listed below are not easy to find out in emerging markets, and in order to come up with the best possible assumption many will require creative research methods.

1 Understanding the market

Companies should be careful not to be misled by statements such as: "There are 1 billion consumers in India. Every one of them is a potential buyer of our TV sets." In reality, most of the 1 billion will be poor and living outside the cash economy at subsistence level. Does this mean there must at least be a few hundred million who can afford to buy what we sell? Not necessarily. There could be a large domestic player dominating the market in such a low pricing range that no foreign company can match it without radically changing its manufacturing cost structure and being prepared to accept lower margins than usual.

It is also important to bear in mind, especially in business-to-business transactions, that demand can be sudden. This is hard to predict. Hence the importance of local presence and building up of relationships so that you have your ears close to the ground and hear about likely developments in the market. Questions to ask about the market are as follows.

Market potential

- How large and wealthy is this market? Calculate local production plus imports minus exports.
- What is the history of local consumption of the product/service?
- What percentage of local production is actually sold? How much is lying around unsold?
- Is there unsatisfied demand for the product/service?
- Are there any re-export dynamics that should be considered?
- How important are parallel or grey imports (smuggled or counterfeit)?
- What has traditionally driven local consumption of the product/service?
- What are the current and likely future drivers of local consumption?
- How is local consumption likely to evolve in the next 5–10 years?

Understanding local consumers/customers

- Who are the consumers/customers? What are their characteristics?

- What do consumers/customers want? Interview buyers and dealers/distributors for preferences.
- Where are they in the country in question? Where are the clusters or pockets of purchasing power?
- How do consumers/customers make their decisions?
- What are their spending patterns?
- How much money do they have to spend?
- How do other companies in the sector see the customer/consumer base and how much are they able to sell to them in reality?

Reaching the consumer/customer
- How difficult/easy is it to reach potential consumers/customers?
- Who are the potential local selling partners that need to be engaged?
- How do competitors and non-competitors reach their customers?
- Who can help with contacting potential partners?
- What are the most effective ways to promote the product?
- What kind of advertising/promotion works best?

Competition
- Which competitors are already operating in the market (both international and local)?
- If local competitors are important players, how sustainable is their existence and what is it based on? Is there a danger of smaller local competitors playing a stronger role in the future?
- How strong are competitors that are already there?
- How many people do they employ and what is their organisational structure?
- Are other competitors entering or planning to enter the market?
- What do customers/consumers think about competitors and their products/services?
- What have been competitors' experiences and results, both negative and positive, in the local market?
- If competitors failed, why?
- If competitors succeeded, why?

Understanding lessons learned by non-competitors
- What do non-competitors say about the business environment in the country?

- ◪ What have been the largest obstacles to successful operations?
- ◪ How can such obstacles be overcome, if at all?
- ◪ What is the discrepancy between official statistics and actual achievable sales? In other words, is there more purchasing power/money in the country than the official statistics suggest?
- ◪ What level of local resources is necessary to avoid the risk of under-penetrating the market or under-exploiting its potential? (See Chapter 7.)

Local culture
- ◪ What specific aspects of local culture are relevant to running a successful local business?
- ◪ What makes this market different from others in the region? Always remember that markets are different and should be examined separately.

2 Understanding the political and economic environment

Questions to ask about the political and economic environment are as follows. (See Chapter 6 for how to interpret economic indicators and Chapter 5 for more on political risk.)

Economic outlook
- ◪ How sustainable is economic growth?
- ◪ What is driving economic growth?
- ◪ How accurate are the relevant economic indicators?
- ◪ Even if reasonably accurate, are economic growth indicators misleading when it comes to local consumption, and why?
- ◪ If real economic growth is likely, will this mean that GDP per head will also increase?
- ◪ What will happen to the exchange rate and inflation rate?
- ◪ What is the likelihood of devaluation or depreciation and how large could it be?
- ◪ What are the stories and assumptions behind other economic indicators that may have an impact on operations?
- ◪ How independent is the local central bank? Are its policies shaped by politics rather than sound principles of monetary management?

Political outlook
- ◪ What is the level of political risk and how will or might it affect the business?

◪ What is the risk and what kind of companies will be most affected by it? For example, is it only those with a large asset investment on the ground that are at risk?

◪ What subtler forms of political risk (see below) could affect operations?

Government policies and their impact on business

◪ Does the government allow a level playing field? Is there discrimination against international companies? If yes, potentially how disadvantageous or dangerous could this discrimination be for the business?

◪ Is the government in the hands of local lobbies and to what extent do local special-interest groups have a detrimental influence on business?

◪ Does the government protect intellectual property?

◪ Does the government encourage free trade? Does it allow and even encourage non-tariff barriers?

◪ Is the government trustworthy when dealing with foreign companies?

◪ Does the government protect private property and how high is the risk of expropriation?

◪ To what extent does the government interfere with pricing?

◪ What is the government record in implementing antitrust policies?

◪ What is the quality of public administration and government bureaucracy?

◪ Is it an effective and efficient government to deal with or is it ineffective and inefficient?

◪ How quick is policy formulation and execution?

◪ Who are the key government players at the federal, regional and city levels that can make or break plans for a business?

◪ How open is the government to foreign involvement in the economy? Does it encourage and even provide incentives for foreign investment?

◪ What kind of local organisation is allowed?

3 Understanding the business environment

Questions to ask about the business environment are as follows.

Finance
- Is it possible to finance operations locally or will it be necessary to rely on in-company finance or sources from abroad?
- What access do customers/consumers have to finance?
- What are the loan conditions for different types of firms and private consumers?
- Can finance be raised through local capital markets (corporate bonds or equity)?
- How stable is the banking system? How high is the risk of collapse and how good/bad is banking supervision?
- How efficient is the banking system?
- Are banks willing to lend money to local private individuals, small and medium-sized enterprises and large domestic companies?
- Is it possible to repatriate profits freely and is the currency convertible? How difficult is it to move funds in and out of the country?
- Is it easy or difficult to transfer money within the country?
- What other potential sources of funding (development banks, government agencies, and so on) can be tapped into for the project?
- Are there any potential local partners who might co-finance the project?

Labour market
- What are the wage/salary rates for the employees who will be needed?
- How high are social security contributions and what is the outlook for them?
- Is the labour market hot (is there a lot of poaching) or not? What is the outlook?
- How educated is the labour force?
- How unionised is the local labour force? What is the incidence of strikes?
- What are the main weaknesses of the labour force? Which areas will require most training?
- What are the most effective ways of recruiting local employees?
- How flexible or inflexible is labour law and what is the outlook for it?

Taxation
- What are the current levels of taxation?
- What are the planned changes to the tax system?
- What kind of "less obvious/hidden taxes" exist in the market?
- What kind of tax holidays and incentives exist at national, regional and city levels?
- What is the outlook for tax incentives?
- How frequent are tax inspections and are they carried out fairly?
- What kind of organisational structure/legal entity is the most advantageous in terms of taxation and local cost structure?

Legal environment
- How effective and efficient is the local judiciary?
- Can foreign companies rely on local commercial courts?
- Is arbitration the best option and where should it take place?
- What is the discrepancy between laws on paper and actual implementation?
- Is there a discrepancy between interpretation of the same laws from province to province or from city to city?
- Is there any hope that the local legal system will improve? If yes, how long will the process last?

Bureaucratic obstacles to business
- What are the most common bureaucratic obstacles for business (permits, licences, and so on)?
- How easy or difficult it is to move goods through customs?
- How easy or difficult it is to set up business in the country? How long does it take and what is required?

Crime and corruption
- Is crime a problem for business?
- Is organised crime a problem for business?
- Does crime or organised crime affect only local companies or does it also affect foreign players?
- What kind of crime is problematic for business?
- What should a security policy cover?
- How are other companies fighting a crime problem? Is the problem manageable?
- What is the level of corruption? How does it affect business? Is it getting better or worse?

- Who is corrupt? Which individuals and which government institutions?

Infrastructure
- What is the quality of local transport infrastructure?
- What is the quality of local telecommunications infrastructure?

Foreign trade environment
- Is the country a member of the World Trade Organisation? If it is, how closely does it follow WTO rules?
- Does it belong to any trading blocs or regional free-trade areas?
- Which bilateral free-trade agreements does it have?
- What is the outlook for any future free-trade agreements?
- Do these signed free-trade agreements work in practice? If they do not, what are the problems?
- Are non-tariff barriers significant and what is the outlook in that regard?
- Are there customs bottlenecks and how much would they add to operational costs?
- Is there a problem of illegal/parallel imports (or even counterfeit products)?

Current and future cost of building a business and brand
Estimating the cost of expanding in or entering an emerging market is difficult and frequently underestimated by multinational companies. The most common mistake is to underestimate the time needed to accomplish an action plan. Even the simplest task (for example, getting a stamp on a permit) that would take a few hours in most developed countries can take days or weeks in an emerging market. Companies need to take time during this preparatory stage to understand how long it will realistically take. After all, time is money.

- How expensive is the operational environment and what is the outlook?
- How expensive is it to build a brand and what is the outlook for advertising prices?
- How much time will it take to do what is necessary to get the business off the ground?

The internal audit

Detailed and continuous understanding of the external environment is just one part of the challenge when setting up and running an emerging-market operation. The other is assessing the internal capabilities needed to match market requirements.

The internal audit prepares managers for the internal battle for corporate resources by assessing in detail what is needed to develop business opportunities effectively and to minimise the risks identified during the external research. If an internal audit results in the allocation of adequate resources, the likelihood of business success will jump dramatically.

Most of the emerging markets with obvious potential have now passed the point where strong and profitable market positions can be established without significant investment of resources.

The key questions to ask in an internal audit are as follows.

- What is needed? If this market opportunity is developed systematically, how much time and money will be required?
- Are the CEO and senior management committed to supporting a systematic business development and providing the necessary resources? Note that the commitment of the CEO is sometimes not enough; other senior managers also have to support the project.
- Is the product portfolio right for the market?
- Which existing products have the strongest chance of success?
- Can the business opportunity identified be addressed by existing products and services? Or does the product/service portfolio need broadening to match the needs of local consumers/customers?
- If market research suggests that the product portfolio is wrong for the market, will investment be available for developing new products?
- Would a modest modification of the current portfolio of products/services do the trick or is something entirely new needed?
- If substantial changes to the product/service portfolio are needed, would this deviate too much from the core strategy? How long would it take to make the changes and how much would it cost?
- What human resources are needed? Is there enough internal human resource expertise to develop the business in these complex markets or will it have to be acquired? What is the view

of the human resources department about all HR issues?

◪ Are processes and structures flexible enough and adequate for what is planned? Will existing internal processes and operational practices help or hinder what is planned? (Many companies give more flexibility to their emerging-market business teams because they have found that structures that work well in mature markets are often too slow and inflexible to respond to day-to-day challenges in emerging markets. The internal audit should identify what operational aspects need to be addressed before going ahead.)

◪ What existing capacities can be drawn on?

◪ What existing internal strengths can usefully be built on? For example, before entering the Russian market, one firm realised that it could ship products duty-free from its plant in Kenya to Russia because of an old free-trade agreement. This circumvented enormously high import duties and made a crucial contribution to the success of the business over the years. Many multinationals have used Austrian employees to expand operations into eastern Europe, believing that they are culturally better positioned to establish successful operations than people who grew up in, say, Ohio.

◪ Is there pressure/encouragement from customers to expand?

◪ Can the risks that have been identified be managed? Are the internal structure, processes and people up to managing financial and other risks the business will face? (Identifying potential risks is not the same as having the capability to manage them.)

◪ How would entry be financed? Are the funds available, and if not, how would they be raised? Are there development bank funds or incentive schemes that can be tapped into? Should the cost of expansion be shared with local partners?

After examining their internal capabilities, most companies realise that there is a resource gap which needs to be addressed. Some companies invest time and money to close it and some do not. The latter generally fail.

The next step is a business proposal, based on the external and internal analyses, to senior management. It includes what to do, how to do it and by when, as well as a detailed outline of resource requirements.

4 Market research and business intelligence

Few things foul us up quicker than bad information.

Mort Crim, veteran American broadcaster

Collecting business intelligence in emerging markets is trickier, more demanding and more time-consuming than in developed markets. This chapter explains how to conduct complex research, how to save money doing it, and which methods and sources to use.

Market research takes more time in emerging markets than in developed markets and the outcome of intelligence gathering is often disappointing. In the majority of emerging markets, data are often unreliable, vague and hard to find. Needless to say, this makes senior management and everyone else involved nervous. How can a company make a sound and potentially costly business decision on partially accurate and incomplete information?

There are two ways for emerging market managers to minimise the risks. First, they should rely more on primary research than on secondary research wherever possible. Primary research means going straight to the source, in many cases through interviews with potential customers and other companies. Carrying out primary research in emerging markets is time-consuming and is not cheap. One multinational conducted more than 50,000 interviews with potential customers to improve its market intelligence before entering a cluster of new markets. Benchmarking against companies which devote substantial resources to research is critical. There are many companies willing to spend tens of millions of dollars during implementation which hesitate to spend a fraction of that for the detailed business intelligence research that is essential if they are to understand and succeed in the market they are entering.

A manager who relies solely on desk research is like a ship's captain who sees only the tip of an iceberg; it is the large chunk below the surface that makes or breaks the business. It is this invisible part that business intelligence should focus on most. Desk research is only a start, but it can provide useful background information and basic data. In some instances it will offer some intelligence, but companies should particularly be wary of local media reports, which are often more biased than foreign sources.

Government information sources can also be misleading. For example, a new commercial law may sound good on paper, but what is the chance that it will be implemented and enforced? A reality check with law firms and other players in a market is more important than the letter of the law.

Consultants can help, but since data are scarce and unreliable, market research firms often recycle and repackage old information. In some countries one or two sources are recycled over and over again, often repeating information that is wrong and misleading for decision-making. You have to carry out primary research to find out the realities of the market.

It is also important to realise that leading consulting firms frequently charge top-dollar rates for conducting primary and secondary research, which they then subcontract to local firms. Substantial savings can be made by going direct to consulting firms which focus on specific sectors or regions.

Qualitative inputs – or gut feelings

The risks of poor market research can also be greatly reduced by devoting resources to qualitative inputs. Many business decisions in emerging markets will to a large extent be based on instinct and gut feeling, and there are two ways to ensure that such instincts and feelings are more than guesswork.

One way is to have a small team of people in charge of co-ordinating business information gathering and analysis. An efficient and quick-witted internal business intelligence team keeps a company sharp and ready to act and react appropriately. This is crucial to staying ahead of the competition, as it means managers are kept up to date with analysis of the business environment and are better able to anticipate any emerging risks and opportunities. These teams can help gather and share information on a regional basis; they can also pass on information and intelligence from one emerging market that could be relevant in another. People hired to run such co-ordination centres have to be good analysts. They should be able to say: "Based on this information, this is the implication for our business and this is why." *Although diss.in multinational context*

The other way to develop reliable instincts is through networking. Building up a good network of contacts and maintaining them is the most powerful business intelligence tool in emerging markets. It is as important for companies entering the market for the first time as it is for those already established, since personal relationships matter much more than in developed markets. Networks provide business intelligence that is unavailable through conventional research. They can help with all aspects of external market analysis as well as with benchmarking how internal assessments were made and how internal resource gaps were closed. They add more comfort to decision-making and decrease the chance of failure.

A business network is a base for continuous benchmarking. Are we underinvesting relative to the competition and by how much? Are we on the right track? Is everyone else facing this complicated issue (meaning that it is not our fault, but a feature of a difficult market)? Are we taking the right steps to try to resolve a problem or is our approach different from other players in the market? All these questions are difficult to answer in any other way.

Personal contact is crucial in all aspects of networking. Business in most emerging markets is intensely personal. Many managers are ignored by government officials and potential partners, suppliers or customers because of a lack of personal bonding. Many companies make the mistake of replacing their expatriate managers every few years, thus damaging their local business. The same goes for retaining key local staff, since when they leave they take their personal relationships with them.

Different kinds of networks are important in emerging markets. The most important are described below.

Peer groups

The best stories about emerging markets are never published; they are told over dinner and during coffee breaks at meetings of regional and country managers. Joining regional and local peer groups and associations provides easy access to useful knowledge. In emerging markets, managers from competing companies often socialise and discuss how to handle generic business issues. The challenges these managers face are so overwhelming that both sides benefit from sharing information and insights.

Government networks

Government policies can be difficult to follow and understand even in advanced emerging markets. At worst, new laws may be applied before the new legislation has been announced.

Most successful companies in emerging markets have an external affairs team comprising managers who are mainly in charge of developing and maintaining links to authorities. Their job is to understand how government policy is shaped and to anticipate any legislative changes that might affect the business. They must also know who is influencing important commercial laws and regulations at all levels of government. This requires relationships with ministers and their deputies and advisers, as well as the lower-level bureaucrats with whom companies have regular dealings.

Other important personal business intelligence contacts
These include the following.

- Existing customers, suppliers and business partners, as well as potential ones.
- Leading analysts and opinion leaders who regularly follow the market and generally know more than they publish. Extracting their intimate knowledge of the market and its challenges is invaluable.
- Influential local businessmen, especially where they have a major influence on government policy and the business environment. Such contacts can help bring substantial additional business. But it can all backfire if the regime changes and your contact is not in favour with the new one. Achieving a balance that allows a company to get the most benefit from its contacts while not exposing it too much should the climate change is a challenge that has to be weighed on a case-by-case basis.
- Business conferences featuring good debates between government officials and business. Networking at events is also important.

Developing a personal knowledge network is neither cheap nor easy, but it is invaluable and goes hand in hand with having strong local presence. It takes patience, time and corporate dedication, but it is as least as important as spending time and money on more conventional research methods. Emerging-market companies need to budget sufficiently for this purpose on a continuous basis.

5 Assessing political risks

You miss 100% of the shots you never take.

Wayne Gretzky, the greatest ice hockey player

There is more business in supposedly dangerous places than many companies imagine. Companies that understand how to interpret the real political risk greatly improve their chances of being among the first to operate profitably in emerging markets. This chapter shows how companies should go about interpreting and assessing political risk. "Only bullets and bombs can prevent our trucks from reaching the consumer," says one Coke bottler. Coca-Cola and some other companies (but not too many) sell their products in some of the most dangerous and politically risky countries in the world. Many writers label Kazakhstan as one of the countries with the highest political risk in the world and not worth doing business in. At the same time, one multinational in the consumer goods business has 120 staff in Almaty, Kazakhstan, and its business (top and bottom line) has doubled in three years with very good profit margins.

Most political risks are irrelevant if a consumer wants to buy and can pay, and physical delivery is possible. But political risks, even minor ones, can and do disrupt business planning. It is from this perspective that companies need to understand and monitor them.

The first step is to make a distinction between political risks that affect sales and those that affect investments in physical assets on the ground. Many multinational companies have ignored good sales opportunities because their political risk analysis dominated their overall market assessment. The perception of high political risk hijacked their thinking and limited their sales activities.

International media often heighten the sense of political risk. Companies that are only interested in selling to a market need to look carefully at what is behind the headline news and decide whether the bad news is really bad for sales. Take, for example, the war in the Russian province of Chechnya. Although undoubtedly a great human tragedy, its real influence on business was virtually zero. Most Moscow-based managers would not give it a second thought if media reports had not encouraged their bosses to ask: "Do we need to worry about this?" and "Why are we still doing business in Russia?" The same goes for headlines about India and Pakistan when disputes flare up between the two countries. But is any multinational really pulling out of India?

Interestingly, there are examples of companies investing in physical assets even in very dangerous places. They take a calculated and strategic risk. Most companies do not have the stomach or leadership vision to do this. But it can be done and risks can be minimised. When Coca-Cola built a bottling plant in Angola, for example, rebel forces were still regularly attacking government forces. Shooting occurred not far from the bottling plant. Coca-Cola shared the risk of investment with other partners; it invested in security, keeping the investment low enough for it not to be a catastrophic loss if the facility was destroyed. In such ventures, the downside is a loss of several million dollars and the upside is reasonable sales in the short term and market leadership.

In some ways, the decision on whether to enter a high-risk market is simple because the reality is stark and the expectations are more likely to be realistic. For those who have the stomach and corporate tolerance for calculated risk (for the sake of establishing strategic market leadership), investing in physical assets and establishing operations in a high-risk emerging market may result in a firm becoming the market leader. Equally, it may result in every dollar spent on the project being lost with little warning.

Subtle, less visible political risks – common to most emerging markets – are in many ways more dangerous, and companies need to invest time and money in understanding them. Those that ignore them generally end up facing unpleasant and costly surprises.

Unlevel playing fields

Government discrimination in favour of local players – sometimes blatant and sometimes subtle – is one problem for foreign companies in emerging markets. For example, a large brewery invested more than $100m in breweries in the Czech Republic. But it found it was losing market share to local competitors, which were lowering their prices because they knew they would receive government subsidies to cover any losses. When the company entered the market it knew the subsidies existed but had been told by the government that they were being phased out.

Sometimes a government is influenced by local business groups, which shape the business environment in their own interests. One firm, for example, set up an office in a market with the aim of establishing a network of petrol stations. Its strategy was to import high-quality petrol because the petrol produced by local refineries was low quality and, over the long term, detrimental to car engines. After the company had committed substantial resources to the project, the government, responding to pressure from the local oil monopoly, introduced quality controls on imported oil. The cost of securing quality approval was set at such a level that the foreign company could not compete and, after lobbying the government for months, it pulled out.

• This example illustrates how local firms can team up with governments and damage the business of foreign companies. But it also shows that the foreign company was neither properly prepared to enter the market nor really committed to it. If it had been, it would not have pulled out so quickly after facing its first large obstacle. Eight months later, under pressure from two other foreign companies, the government was forced to abandon its quality control scheme. The company that pulled out is a large player in the United States and Europe but tiny in most emerging markets; this is not surprising given its weak market entry approach.

The interplay between special interest groups and government can take many shapes and forms, but it is a risk that can be anticipated with proper research and, hopefully, it can be dealt with. Companies with or planning operations in emerging markets should have a permanent external affairs team.

Disrespect for intellectual property

Subtle government protection of local companies can take place through slack intellectual property laws. Foreign pharmaceuticals companies operating in Slovenia, for example, have complained for years that local companies steal and copy their formulas. But companies claim that the local courts do not allow foreign experts to testify and none of the local experts wants to appear. "Stealing continues," said a manager of a large multinational. This is in a market that is seen as quite sophisticated and close to developed world standards.

In extreme cases, governments openly support the theft of intellectual property. The International Music Industry Association complained recently, for example, that the government of Ukraine was actively involved in the production of pirated music, even providing the factory space. It is not just obvious sectors such as software and pharmaceuticals that suffer. Master Foods found that its cat food was copied in some countries by counterfeit manufacturers which were so sophisticated that they even had bar codes on the packaging. Tracing such manufacturers is hard and requires huge commitment, and sometimes – a fact the copiers no doubt play on – the cost of chasing them is difficult to justify considering the size of a local market.

Political correctness and autocratic regimes

How risky is it to deal with autocrats or, worse, outright dictators? It depends on whether the regime is supported by the West or not. Dealing with the Suharto regime in Indonesia, for example, brought significant benefits for foreign business interests. Dealing with regimes that are not supported by the West is a questionable strategy. Both types exert direct control over their economies. Many companies are afraid to be associated with "evil" regimes and feel that negative western public perception of their involvement outweighs the benefits of doing business there. Others argue that their involvement is helping the country's economic, social and political development.

Government trustworthiness

As a rule, companies should be at least mildly sceptical when listening to government promises. There are governments that mislead companies intentionally, and there are those that mean what they say but are unable to implement the promises. The best thing that companies can do is to study the previous record of government promises and understand the current political set up. Even in countries with a good track record, the external affairs team should keep the pressure on with regard to changes that are desired and changes that have been promised but not delivered.

An economic crisis may not be bad for business

Bad and inefficient politics have contributed to many economic crises and to many corporate frustrations. But many companies (not publicly, of course) love economic crises and devaluations. This includes companies that manufacture locally and export (now cheaply manufactured goods) mostly to the developed world and companies seeking to buy local assets.

Respect the power of provincial and city authorities

Regional governors and/or city mayors are usually important for business, sometimes even more than federal authorities. As ever, companies should have a clear and detailed understanding of the previous record of such individuals and act accordingly.

What's yours is now not

The risk of property being expropriated or nationalised was serious a few decades ago in a number of countries, but it has clearly diminished. Still, it should not be ignored. When times get desperate so can government actions, as the expropriation of property in Zimbabwe under Robert Mugabe has shown.

Barriers to trade

Despite widespread membership of the World Trade Organisation (146 countries in mid-2003) and the growth in regional trading blocs, some countries are openly protectionist in certain ways. Trading barriers are significantly lower than a few decades ago. Tariff barriers have been cut or removed in many instances, but the use of non-tariff barriers persists in ways that can be complex and infuriating. Examples range from overnight import taxes or import surcharges to imposing quality controls that are either prohibitively expensive or highly complex and time-consuming. All undermine smooth business and profitability and sometimes even price companies out of the market.

A classic example of a non-tariff barrier in the developed world is when the French government tried to stop imports of Japanese video recorders by requiring all VCRs to enter France through one small customs entry point. And there is the continuing saga of agricultural subsidies in the United States and the EU. Although non-tariff barriers are more likely to be introduced in tough economic times, this may also occur when a local industrial or state lobby is strong.

Companies should understand how the government has behaved recently and how it is likely to behave in future. Certain signs potentially indicate more protectionism: for example, if a country's current account deficit is deteriorating, it is likely that the government will need to reduce imports (which can be achieved by quickly raising import barriers) by, for example, introducing an import tax (which the WTO usually tolerates for a limited period in certain circumstances – typically a high current-account deficit or similar macroeconomic imbalance).

Pricing interference

Pharmaceuticals and utility companies are particularly affected by governments seeking to control prices, but so are tobacco, oil or alcohol manufacturers. For example, when a foreign company bought an electricity distributor in Hungary, the government promised (and agreed contractually) that the investor would be able to gradually raise prices to market levels at a certain percentage a year. But for political reasons the government went back on its word and allowed for only half the agreed annual price increases.

Pharmaceuticals companies are already used to governments that tie reimbursement levels to the price of cheap generics.

Public administration and bureaucracy – more quid than pro

If you want to open a manufacturing plant (greenfield or acquisition) in certain emerging markets you will probably have to fly the members of the state environmental committee to inspect your plant in the West. They will also ask for large daily payments and some will insist that their wives (or "nieces") accompany them. In some countries you have to wait for months to get a stamp on an important document, an exercise that would take a few minutes, hours or at worst a few days in the developed world.

Even if corruption is eliminated, many bureaucracies are still inefficient, largely because of the quality of the people. Governments and the tiny salaries they pay are not magnets for top-notch individuals. Private businesses in emerging markets pay much better and usually attract the best people. Thus many countries end up with low-quality staff in key government positions. They may have good intentions, but often they are of little positive use to foreign companies. As a result, many firms setting up or operating in emerging markets put a lot of time and effort into educating bureaucrats and winning them over.

Inefficient and ineffective government

It is important to be aware of how much government inefficiency impinges on the local economy and diminishes the potential for growth. But even so there are many examples of manufacturing companies making good profits in countries run by hopeless governments. For example, if a country is widely perceived as risky, investors can enjoy preferential treatment. When Croatia had a government that few companies wanted to deal with, Ericsson invested some $30m in cash (and some $45m in kind) in manufacturing operations and in return received an exclusive long-term contract (worth at least $500m) to be the sole supplier to the local telecoms monopoly.

When considering more dangerous places, companies often argue that it is too risky to employ people on the ground. The reality is that locals live in dangerous and risky places anyway and are often keen to work. Besides, it is usually possible to find a local distributor.

6 Interpreting economic indicators

Academic economics ... is a primitive science, of course. If you want a parallel, think of medicine at the turn of the century.

Paul Krugman in 1994

Understanding how to interpret often confusing and misleading economic indicators is essential in getting to grips with an emerging market. This chapter explains what each economic indicator means and how it should be interpreted for business purposes. It also highlights the dangers of taking indicators at face value and ignoring the drivers behind them, and it includes examples of how companies have been seriously misled in the past.

Economic performance can never be perfectly measured. Economic indicators do a good job in measuring it, but in most emerging markets the indicators are much less reliable than those for the developed world. Just walk through the streets of Cairo or Mexico City or any rural area in an emerging market and it is clear that unrecorded economic activity is rampant. Turkish or Ukrainian unofficial economic activities are probably as large as official ones.

Even statistics on the official economy are inaccurate, including statistics in developed countries. In developing countries, inaccuracy is typically of much greater magnitude. It is too expensive to collect information on all economic activity, so collection is based on surveys and sampling. As a result, accounts are full of estimates. Many governments distort samples and surveys to produce results that support their political agenda. In many countries there are significant flaws in the data compiling systems.

It is not only a question of lies and bad systems: there are genuine measurement problems. Measurement methodologies have traditionally focused on measuring the output of easy-to-measure physical goods. Few countries, especially in the developing world, bother to measure sectors which have boomed in recent decades, such as information technology, financial services, health care or entertainment. Even if countries try to capture these service industries, it is hard to define what one unit of production really is – which is easy to do if you want to know how many tractors a country produced in a given year. For all countries, accurate statistics are elusive because the share of easy-to-measure manufacturing is shrinking as a proportion of the whole economy. Technological advances often remain unmeasured, which suggests that GDP growth is regularly understated throughout the world.

Where statistics are shaky, economic forecasts are even more uncertain than usual. Remember that forecasters usually publish a main scenario, so it is important to question them about the risks to the scenario and to warn senior management about these before submitting the business plan.

Hints and tips

- ☑ Are the numbers you are looking at real (with the effects of inflation stripped out) or nominal (including inflation)? If they are nominal, look for real.
- ☑ Never judge a situation by a number or two. Look at the past trend and make sure you know what happened before and what is driving current numbers. For example, a country might record high growth rates in a particular year, but this could be because there was a slump in the previous year and the high growth represents catching up rather than a genuine improvement in standards of living.
- ☑ Will the data be subject to later revisions? This especially applies to GDP numbers.
- ☑ Will the data you are looking at be seasonally adjusted? For example, third quarter GDP growth may be boosted by a bumper harvest, but growth over the whole year may be much lower.
- ☑ Don't get excited if a country's GDP rises by 2%. If its population increased by 2.2% in the same period, per head GDP actually declined.

GDP

GDP forecasts are given great weight in many business plans. But this can be misleading. As *The Economist* has said: "GDP should really stand for Grossly Deceptive Product."

GDP: what it is and why you should be careful when using GDP forecasts

GDP is the total market value of all final goods and services produced within an economy in a given year. The quantity of goods is multiplied by prices. Say that an economy produced 50,000 tractors (at a unit price of $20,000) and 20,000 cars (at $25,000 each) in a given year. GDP is thus (50,000 × $20,000) + (20,000 × $25,000) = $1.5 billion. If the prices of tractors and cars grow next year, it will appear that GDP has increased. This would be a nominal increase in GDP.

To calculate real GDP it is necessary to keep prices constant, or in other words adjust for inflation. Take the cars in this example. In year 1 GDP was 20,000 × $25,000 = $500m. In year two production increased to 22,000 cars and the price increased to $26,000, giving GDP of $572m. It appears that GDP rose by 14.4%. But if prices from year one are used to recalculate year 2 (22,000 cars × $25,000), it is clear that real GDP rose to $550m and there was a 10% real increase.

To understand what drives growth or decline in GDP, you need to know who is buying the final goods and services that are produced. Either they are bought by consumers, firms or government, or they are net exports (exports minus imports).

GDP forecasts are an indication of growth in standards of living over the medium to long term. They are also a broad indication of comparative wealth around the world. But companies in the middle of annual budgeting and planning should use GDP forecasts with caution, for three reasons.

- Growth can be "driven" by strong exports or strong government purchases, but this will not help a company selling toothpaste, for example. It can happen that GDP grows strongly because exports are booming, while at the same time consumer spending is declining (perhaps there has been an increase in personal income tax or utility prices).
- The numbers can be insufficient or exaggerated. China, for example, is widely believed to exaggerate its GDP growth figures.
- For emerging markets in particular, GDP is a far from perfect measure of economic activity. It does not count any underground economy (grey or black economy).

An understanding of what drives growth in an emerging market is more useful for business planning than knowing the overall GDP growth number. More important is an understanding of the underlying reasons for growth in, say, private consumption or purchases by firms. Those engaged in budgeting should look for economic forecasters who can tell the story behind the numbers and explain what will drive growth in future.

But companies need to know more than economics for budgeting purposes. For example, in the mid-1990s, Slovakia was run by an autocrat who kept GDP growth in decent shape by borrowing abroad and using a large chunk of funds to pay subsidies to dying enterprises. The sales of international companies were going well. But his policies created high indebtedness and imbalances. The next government had to cut spending to correct macroeconomic fundamentals. Multinationals budgeted more cautiously, but nothing had prepared them for a sudden double-digit decrease in sales. Explaining the drop to senior management was difficult. GDP growth was lower but still around 2%, so why were sales doing so badly? It was because exports were strong and driving growth, while all kinds of domestic consumption (private, corporate and government) were decreasing. The extent of the consumption decline was, in fact, even greater than the statistics showed because of the deficiencies in measurement methodology.

In some countries GDP as a whole is a misleading indicator for business because of the disproportionate influence of certain sectors. Moroccan GDP, for example, rises and falls like a yo-yo depending on the fortunes of the agriculture sector. Oil-dominated economies go through similar peaks and troughs depending on the oil price. In these countries, when looking at GDP estimates, it is important to understand the significance of the dominant sector and how its potential volatility affects sales and business.

It is also important to remember that business and economic cycles in most emerging markets are stronger than those in the developed world. Economic busts can be far more devastating than anyone would expect (see Chapter 14). The same goes for economic booms. Emerging markets have the capacity (if economic policies are run well) to grow at least twice as fast as developed countries.

So what should companies in the planning and budgeting cycle do to avoid being misled by GDP statistics?

- Understand what is driving growth or decline as well as the dynamics behind each driver.
- Identify and monitor the factors that drive sales in specific sectors.
- Benchmark sales and sales projections with competitors.
- Make sure that senior management are aware that GDP growth numbers can be misleading.

Doubling GDP

How do you calculate how long will it take (approximately) for GDP/standards of living to double from current levels? The mathematical formula is 70 divided by an average percentage growth figure for the coming years. For example, if you believe the Chilean economy will grow 4% per year (on average in the next few years), dividing 70 by 4 you arrive at the estimate that it will take 17.5 years for Chilean living standards to double (on average) from current levels. Nice mathematics, but who believes in long-term forecasts?

Current-account deficit

Another indicator to monitor is the current-account deficit. This can act as a warning, highlighting currency weakness or potential changes in economic policy that might affect business.

Current account

The current account is the sum of net exports of goods and services (exports minus imports), net income received from investments abroad (net profits, dividends and rents) and net transfer payments from abroad (things like workers' remittances from abroad).

How does a deficit arise and how might it affect currency values? A current-account deficit is the result of actions that create a demand for foreign currency. Take the biggest chunk of the current account, exports and imports of goods, and assume other components are zero. Imagine that for some reason (large wage increases or a boom in loans, for example) there is a large demand for imported cars in Poland. BMW's distributor in Poland, facing strong demand from customers, has to sell zlotys to buy euros in order to get more cars from BMW in Germany. Now imagine hundreds and thousands of local importers all doing the same because there is booming demand for imported products. What is the net effect on the local currency? The price of it (the exchange rate) can come under pressure as more and more people sell the local currency.

In theory, the balance of payments must balance, so any deficit must be financed by capital inflows. These include foreign direct investment (FDI), international borrowing and the sale of foreign-exchange reserves.

If the current-account deficit exceeds 4% of GDP, it is in the danger zone, according to standard international benchmarks. In other words, there is an increased risk of currency depreciation. In practice, it is not so clear-cut. Many emerging markets go over the limit without any obvious effect, and companies should always bear this mind.

One of the reasons is that central banks intervene. They sell foreign reserves and buy local currency to stop currency depreciation (or vice versa if they are fighting a rising currency). This is why it is important to look at the value of foreign-exchange reserves (gold and foreign-currency reserves held by the country) to gauge whether a high current-account deficit spells devaluation. The rule of thumb is that reserves should cover at least the value of three months of imports. If they do not or are declining, this suggests potential difficulties for any central bank wanting to intervene to support the currency.

Another buffer for current-account deficits is FDI. If investment flows are high and rising and cover a large proportion of the deficit, the currency is in no danger (unless market psychology says it is). Foreign investment is a healthy way to cover the current-account gap. It will probably lead to improved exports, which should over time reduce the deficit and lead to better, sustainable economic growth.

The other variable is the reliability of other capital flows: access to international borrowing at an acceptable price; workers' remittances, which play a huge role in economies such as Turkey and India; and other foreign-exchange earners, such as the Suez Canal in Egypt. It is important to know whether the imports that are creating an imbalance are largely consumer goods inflows or capital goods inflows. A large proportion of capital goods indicates that industry is retooling, which will result in higher exports over time. In other words, capital goods imports are healthier for economic stability than consumer goods imports.

Taken all together, a country with poor access to international financing, low inflows of FDI and low or declining foreign-exchange reserves is more likely to face a currency crisis if it has a large current-account deficit. But in many cases, even that does not have to push a currency into collapse. Many African countries, for example, fit the description perfectly but are kept afloat by donor and multilateral financing, often from the IMF and World Bank.

As with other indicators, it is important to know the story behind the current-account deficit in order to assess its true riskiness. But even if the analysis shows that the risks are not dramatic, high deficits often bring changes in economic policy that might affect sales. Central banks may raise interest rates, for example, to cut demand for imports (and so reduce the current-account deficit). Or governments may impose an import tax or import surcharge to achieve the same effect. Both measures can easily reduce sales in a country.

Short-term capital-account flows – hot money, hot flushes

Capital-account flows have become increasingly important as an indicator of potential dangers for local currencies in many emerging economies (see Chapter 14). The deficit on the capital account arises from actions that result in a growing demand for foreign currency. Hot money is a popular name for short-term capital movements. These include investments in liquid assets such as Treasury bills and bank deposits, but most economists now also include portfolio investment in stocks and bonds under the hot money label. A change in market sentiment from positive to negative can result in sudden outflows of these liquid investments and that weakens the domestic currency. Country managers need to observe hot-money inflows and evaluate the likelihood of sudden outflows. Some countries regularly experience large inflows while market sentiment is positive and then sudden outflows as it turns negative. These tidal movements can easily create a series of seemingly unstoppable crises, as any manager running a Turkish operation will know.

Budget deficits

The fiscal policies and budgets of emerging economies often attract headline attention. A deficit is when expenditure is higher than revenue and is reconciled by borrowing or, if the government is unable to borrow, by printing money. The latter is the road to hyperinflation. Managers need to be well aware of the government's ability to borrow in order to assess potential risk for hyperinflation.

Another potential danger of the budget deficit is that it accumulates and future generations will have to pay higher taxes to finance it. To gauge this risk, look at the level of government debt as a percentage of GDP. Government debt is the sum of all government deficits over the years. A large accumulation of debt increases interest payments, which add to the budget deficit.

By boosting demand for money, budget deficits lead to higher interest rates and these "crowd out" private investment. Funds are redirected to the government, starving local businesses of finance with which to boost productivity and living standards. The size of the impact depends on various factors; for example, countries with a higher savings rate absorb deficits more easily than those with low savings rates.

To cover budget deficits, central banks sometimes buy government securities (new issues and existing debt) issues. This is called monetising, but it is nothing more than the government borrowing from the central bank, or in effect printing money, since new money enters into circulation. It is important to look out for operations like these because they often lead to high inflation. In former Yugoslavia in the early 1990s it led to hyperinflation of several trillion per cent which could only be stopped by reducing the excessive budget deficit.

Off-budget funds are another favourite way of hiding deficits. Developed countries have them too, but they are common in most emerging markets, giving a prettier picture for the "official" deficit. To get the full picture, you need to add the official numbers and the off-budget funds to get a consolidated budget deficit figure. Off-budget funds may not be transparent. People who track countries on a daily basis can estimate what they might be (and their size), and some countries do say which funds are treated off-budget.

Government debt approaching 60% of GDP and rising is considered worrying for emerging economies. Developed economies often carry higher percentages and still avoid major difficulties. As a rule of thumb, the danger signals are rising government debt accompanied by low domestic investment by firms and individuals and rising inflation.

Headline news about budget deficits is often misleading. The Czech Republic, for example, has a budget deficit of 10% of GDP. This sounds worrying until you realise that government debt is low by international standards at less than 40% of GDP.

Deficit creation is not always bad news. A temporary increase in public spending to pull an economy out of recession is fine, especially if the overall government debt is within acceptable international standards. International financial institutions often tell emerging-market governments to tighten their belts during a regular, cyclical economic downturn. But this generally makes the downturn worse, turning small economic downturns into large ones (see Chapter 14).

Many countries end up running deficits on both the budget and the current account at the same time. Watching for twin deficits – or their potential emergence – is useful for business planning. Governments facing this double squeeze are often forced into austerity measures: reducing imports, cutting fiscal spending, raising interest rates to reduce local demand, and so on. For most companies, this means a substantial reduction in sales for one or two years.

Inflation

The inflation rate is a percentage rate of change in price levels, based on an average of all the prices in an economy. These days annual inflation of 2–3% is considered natural and acceptable. In inflationary times people have an incentive to spend since money does not hold its value. Prices change quickly, causing confusion about true value. The consumer price index (CPI) is the most common indicator used to follow inflationary trends. Like other indicators it is not perfect, being based on a basket of different goods and services used by a supposedly typical household – and this basket is determined by governments. If they want to show low inflation, for example, the basket may include goods supported by government subsidies. It is good to be aware of these games before relying on official inflation figures.

Inflation

Inflation can be demand-pull or cost-push. Demand-pull inflation is frequently referred to as "too much money chasing too few goods". Prices go up when demand exceeds availability. Demand (purchasing power) can be pushed up by a number of factors: a credit boom (more borrowing), tax cuts, increased government spending, or wages rising faster than productivity (maybe because there are labour shortages).

Cost-push inflation arises from price shocks. They can include sudden jumps in commodity and raw materials prices (as happens sometimes with oil), or a weaker domestic currency can make imports more expensive (as happened following the introduction of the euro).

Hyperinflation (a term widely accepted to mean inflation exceeding 50% per month) is a result of high money-supply growth (usually linked to an inability to borrow to cover a large budget deficit).

High inflation is bad for business. It distorts real values and corporate behaviour. Companies operating in emerging markets have developed sophisticated inflation accounting standards. But inflation is hard to predict and uncertainty about it discourages investments.

Interest rates

Central bankers pay a lot of attention to the inflation rate. If it exceeds the level of nominal interest rates, the real interest rate becomes negative. This discourages savings, which means there is less money available for lending and for spending on capital goods, which in turn might eventually lead to a fall in living standards. Occasionally, where an economic downturn coincides with currency strength (as in the Czech Republic in 2002, for example), central banks allow temporary negative rates in an attempt to reduce the value of the currency and stimulate economic growth. But in emerging markets the typical reaction to economic downturns is to raise interest rates sharply and suddenly (see Chapter 14).

This is the opposite of what happens in developed markets and the impact on business can be enormous. Central banks in emerging markets have a tendency to increase rates too much too quickly to calm the financial markets. To be aware of possible sharp interest-rate hikes, you need to develop a good feel for the psychology of the market and always distinguish between nominal rates (those quoted in the market) and real rates. Subtracting the actual inflation rate from a nominal rate will give you the real interest rate.

Exports

The structure of exports indicates the overall health of the economy. If an economy is heavily dependent on exports of commodities or semi-finished products, it is much more likely to be affected by swings in world prices and there will be little it can do to avoid a slowdown or even a crisis. Data on export structures are available for all countries and are a good indicator of sustainable economic strength. It is also useful to know where exports are heading. For example, if Germany is in trouble this is immediately felt in central Europe because Germany is the most important import destination for countries such as Poland, Hungary and the Czech Republic.

A useful indicator for companies to track is the value of exports from various areas of a country. This can expose unexpected pockets of hard currency. For example, contrary to expectations that "there is little outside of Moscow and St Petersburg", there are prosperous companies and consumers in Russia's oil and diamond exporting regions.

Official reserves and currency interventions

The official reserves of a country include all foreign currency and gold held by governments. Governments should have at least enough reserves to cover three months of imports. The reserves are used for currency interventions and to pay for any international obligations. Any rapid fall in reserves is a possible sign of intervention to stop the currency depreciating. A rapid rise in reserves may indicate that the central bank wants to stop the currency appreciating in value. Note that many countries in emerging markets overestimate the gold value of their reserves.

One important impact on business of a currency intervention that aims to stop depreciation (selling foreign reserves and buying local currency to increase the demand for the latter) is that the money supply shrinks, which may have an impact on domestic demand and liquidity and ultimately sales. But the amount of local currency in circulation will increase if the central bank is trying to stop the currency appreciating in value. To avoid the inflationary effect of a higher money supply, central banks "mop up" excess supply by selling government bonds to the public.

External debt and the ability to service it

External debt includes debt owed by both the private and the public sector. Deficits on the current account result in accumulation of external debt, the interest payments on which and the repayments of which can be financed only by income earned from exports. It is important to keep an eye on payment schedules. It is not difficult to identify the critical periods in the next few years when debt repayments will be particularly large. The next stage is to assess the ability of the country to meet such obligations (service the debt). There are many emerging markets with a potential debt repayment problem which could turn into a crisis.

7 Eternal dilemmas: market entry, corporate structure, marketing

We realise now that micro-managing from a distance does not work.

Sir Terry Leahy, CEO of Tesco

You own these businesses. Take charge of them. Get headquarters out of your hair. Fight the bureaucracy. Hate it. Kick it. Break it.

Jack Welch, former CEO of General Electric

Companies need a centre that is strong without being crushing and outposts that are true to themselves without losing our corporate identity.

Rod Eddington, CEO, British Airways

Companies often assume that the product they sell so successfully in the developed world will sell successfully in emerging markets. In practice, this is only partly true. This chapter explains why and explores the latest successful and less successful market entry and marketing approaches employed by multinationals in emerging economies.

Glance at the market shares of many companies from country to country and you will see enormous differences. In some markets they are leaders; in others they are far behind their international and domestic competition. Even large multinationals, which are clearly market leaders in the developed world, sometimes fall far behind smaller international competitors and even tiny domestic companies in some emerging markets. How is that possible?

The explanation can be found in different approaches to market entry and market expansion. Companies such as Coca-Cola and Nestlé, which have exceptionally strong emerging-market operations, demonstrate two crucial traits. First, they have strong commitment from the top to developing long-term dominance in emerging markets. Second, they focus on building up local infrastructure and brands at the time of market entry. They know that getting a strong local presence in place as early as possible lays the foundations for future business success. These two basic prerequisites for building a strong local business sound like common sense. So why do so many companies fail to do it?

As discussed in Chapter 2, the main reason is entrenched short-termist behaviour. The more short-termist the company, the more it is likely to trail behind international and local market leaders in emerging markets – and many trail big time. Most are disappointed and frustrated at the success of their smaller and otherwise weaker competitors who achieve excellent sales, market shares and profits. As emerging markets mature commercially, it will become harder to change market shares, as it is in the developed world.

Reasons for firms failing to secure a strong position in emerging markets include the following.

- No commitment from the top to long-term dominance of emerging markets.
- Minimal or no local presence to support marketing and sales.
- Leaving distributors to run the business on the ground.
- Fly-in, fly-out management of local markets (a regional manager who "lives" on the plane and manages distributors by visits only).
- Leaving distributors without or with little support.
- Limited or no investment in marketing/advertising.

This kind of approach will not work. The company will not develop a deep enough knowledge of the market and customers, and it will not build those crucial personal relationships with authorities, partners and customers. The company will have little control over its business. Sales will be limited by the capacity of importers and distributors (who often have a hard time raising finance at acceptable cost). They may also be limited to certain areas within a country, and it will be hard to develop a strong brand with widespread market reach. So how should it be done?

Local presence

Local presence is crucial to success. Companies need to have a local office focusing on marketing and sales, even when markets are small. How big the initial investment needs to be and when the move should be made are questions of strategy. Companies that focus aggressively on achieving market leadership admit that they "overinvest" initially, although they are aware of the potential retrenchment risk if the fixed-cost base becomes too large during an emerging-market crisis. These companies argue that slight overinvesting is better than underinvesting in local offices, especially while the market is in an earlier business-development stage.

Underinvestment leads to underpenetrating the market: in other words, not fully taking advantage of all the opportunities it presents. As a senior manager at Nike says:

> One of the frequent internal debates we have is whether we have penetrated the market enough or if we are still in the underpenetration stage.

A fear of underpenetrating the market is the driving force behind the overinvestment philosophy. Regardless of how much good market research is done, it is easy to miss some of the business opportunities that exist. Underpenetration results in the competition grabbing more of the local market.

Other, less aggressive, companies wait until sales reach a certain (fairly low) level and then decide to set up a local presence. This can work well as long as the local presence is set up early enough. However, many companies wait too long to get their sales up before going local. Those that adopt this approach usually fall behind the competition.

Getting the corporate structure right

> We tried hard – but it seemed that every time we were beginning to form up into decent teams we would be reorganised by our superiors from above. I was to learn later in life that our organisation tended to meet any situation by reorganising, and what a wonderful method it can be for creating the illusion of progress while in reality producing only confusion, inefficiency and demoralisation.

This was the wise comment of Gaius Petronius, a Roman general who died in AD66, but it could just have well have been a regional manager in a large multinational. While some companies choose inappropriate corporate structures for the emerging market region they are entering and operating in, even more companies damage their businesses by restructuring frequently.

Some of those operating in emerging markets turn a full circle. They start heavily centralised to save costs and dip a toe into the market. Then they realise they need to be more decentralised to do business effectively. After a while, they start focusing on rapidly rising costs as the business grows, so they centralise again – all in less than five years. No wonder many regional managers complain that they have no time to run the business. Frequent changes in organisational structure are among the top time-wasters for regional managers. Sometimes the restructuring is a response to changes on the ground, but usually it is initiated by a change of corporate leadership or stock price pressures.

Before setting up a structure or restructuring the old one, companies should ask themselves a fundamental question: what is the structure that will best and fully address the opportunities that exist in the group of emerging economies that it wishes to "conquer"? Here are some recommendations.

Make sure that the CEO supports the emerging-market business
The head of global emerging-markets operations should be close to and supported by the CEO. This is the best way to give emerging-markets business enough push and commitment and to get a fair and proper hearing at the top.

Make sure that each region has its own boss
Each emerging-market region needs its own head manager reporting to the global emerging-markets director and/or the global emerging-markets business unit director. Emerging markets can be divided into three regions: Latin America, Asia (excluding Japan) and Central Eastern Europe, Middle East and Africa (CEEMEA). Some companies break these down further and have regional heads for central Europe, Russia and the CIS, China, South-East Asia, Middle East and North Africa (MENA), Sub-Saharan Africa, and Latin America. This breakdown is fine for a market approach, but the plethora of regional bosses generally makes it more difficult to get the region on to the radar screens of the CEO and senior management. If the regions are large, it is easier to get a proper hearing at the top. Central and eastern Europe, for example, represents some 4% of global GDP. But add to that the Middle East and Africa, and the market size of the region almost doubles.

Don't give a developed-market head the additional responsibility for emerging markets
Those in charge of developed markets (especially large ones) should not be in charge of emerging markets at the same time. For most companies, emerging markets represent low-volume and high-growth business, whereas developed countries represent high-volume and

low-growth business. As discussed throughout this book, the business issues in emerging markets are different, requiring greater flexibility and speed of decision-making, more time, patience and perseverance. Because of this, many multinationals operating in Asia, for example, separate the Japanese operation from the emerging markets in the Asia-Pacific region. This is the right approach. The Japanese market is so huge in itself that the Japan manager barely has time to keep that market going, let alone focus attention on new developments in Vietnam or Indonesia. Equally, managers in charge of Germany and France should not be given responsibility to develop Russia or Romania. These markets should have a regional head. "Put any emerging market together with Germany and it will die," says a senior regional director of a major IT firm.

It sounds like common sense and American multinationals would not dream of having someone who runs the US market also in charge of Latin America. But if multinationals are in short-termist mode (and many are), they will try to save costs and ask their German manager: "Hans, east of you is a large region. Please go ahead and develop the business." This approach does not work. Hans's focus is Germany. This is where his performance is usually judged. He does not necessarily understand the central and eastern Europe region and its issues and he probably has neither the time nor the inclination to fly to Ukraine to set up a business. As a manager of a large industrial firm points out: "Our regional boss who also runs France thinks of central and eastern Europe only when he has time. And he never has time."

Choose a good location for the regional office
Think of placing a regional office in a hub that offers good tax savings from a corporate and personal standpoint (in addition to good transport links or good quality of life). In Europe, for example, many multinationals choose certain Swiss cantons as a regional head office, saving millions in tax every year.

Consider clusters
Consider clusters rather than having each country manager reporting to a regional head (and also an emerging-market business unit head if there is a matrix structure). These clusters are subregions based on geographical proximity, culture, ways of doing business, commercial market maturity, common distributors, trading links or common language. Many firms, for example, have heads of areas such as North

Africa, the Gulf, South-East Europe, or South Asia. Heads of subregions would have country managers reporting to them and they will report to the regional head (and also the business unit head in case of matrix structures).

Clusters within larger emerging-market regions can operate well, providing something of a halfway house between centralised and decentralised operations. They allow companies to keep a clear focus on local business opportunities, while avoiding the high fixed costs associated with multiple full-service subsidiaries. Typically, clusters will provide shared services for back-office functions such as finance, HR and IT support. Increasingly companies have started relocating shared service units for developed regions in emerging markets too.

Another advantage of clusters is that it gives smaller countries a proper hearing with regional management. If they are presented as a group, their size and sales growth rates attract attention, reducing the risk that they will be neglected when it comes to allocation of resources.

Give managers operational freedom

Country or cluster managers need considerable freedom to operate, hire the right people and decide how budgets are spent. They should be held accountable for the performance in their area. Head offices should not stop a local manager from acting in a way that he thinks will be good for the business. For example, they should not insist on keeping the headcount at a certain level if the local manager thinks hiring an extra person will bring in new business. Head office should simply say: "Go ahead and hire if you are convinced this will help your business; you know it is your neck on the line if you can't show results." Importantly, senior management should understand that it may take several years for the results to become apparent.

Don't centralise the marketing and sales functions

The centre must say what the brand should stand for in principle and provide basic brand guidelines, but the universal brand message needs to be adapted to the specifics of an emerging market. Centralised marketing may save costs, but it is also likely to reduce sales.

Marketing in emerging markets – global versus local

Every major multinational can tell at least one story of a marketing fiasco in an emerging market, and the reason is usually the failure to adapt the product, brand image or advertising to local tastes and sensitivities. It is dangerous to assume that the product you have is truly global. Nestlé's yoghurt tastes sweeter in the Middle East and Nescafé instant coffee varies in strength and bitterness from market to market. Even Coke tastes a bit sweeter in Asia. Try selling big gas-guzzling American cars in central Europe and you will get nowhere; people think they are bad and unreliable.

Localise

The key to designing a successful marketing approach is to adapt all elements of the marketing mix to the local market. The main points to bear in mind are as follows.

- Your products and brands are probably not known. Even if they are, are they perceived in the way you want the customer to perceive them?
- Emerging markets offer opportunities for new positioning. If your product is positioned in one of the lower market segments in the developed world, the lack of recognition and loyalty for that brand in emerging markets offers an opportunity to position it at a higher end and to earn a higher margin (Levi's jeans, Jeep Grand Cherokee, for example).
- You will not know what customers want and need unless you ask many of them in different market segments. Research until you drop.
- The fact that the product is foreign does not mean that it will be liked. In some markets, such as India, it is often the reverse.
- If market research shows you do not have a suitable product for the local market, consider whether it would pay to design new products (or reintroduce ones that are no longer profitable in developed markets).
- Most buyers are likely to be price-sensitive, some extremely so. For many, bargain hunting is a way to survive.
- Some buyers will be very well off and a middle class is growing in emerging markets – this is typically more price-sensitive than the middle class in the developed world.
- Nestlé has 8,000 brands but only one-tenth are registered in more than one country.

Customers may not be susceptible to promotional messages that work in developed markets. They are influenced by local cultures, which shape their habits and preferences.

Next look at the product mix and pricing. One of the worst mistakes a company can make is to assume that its products and brands, part of everyday language in developed markets, are known in the local market. It is more likely they will not be known, and a great deal of effort will need to be put into building brand recognition, brand comprehension, brand image, and brand loyalty and trust.

It is also wrong to assume that global premium brands will be seen as superior to local ones. When Kraft Foods acquired a company in central Europe, for example, its plan was to keep selling the acquired domestic brands for a while but gradually phase them out as sales of Kraft's premium brands took off. As time went by the opposite happened. Local buyers were reluctant to spend money on the more expensive premium brands but liked the better quality Kraft brought to local brands. Sales of these started to grow more rapidly than those of the new premium products. When times are tough, consumers not only become more price-sensitive but also experiment less with their limited funds. They stick to trusted brands.

Many companies have now abandoned the idea of just selling their global brands. Instead they introduce a variety of products for multiple domestic market segments from the cheapest to the most expensive, embracing a mix of global and local products. For other companies, launching new, cheaper products for more price-sensitive market segments is anathema. Their global strategy is to expand sales of their global brands. That is fine, but they will never gain high market shares in emerging markets unless they launch products for price-sensitive consumers. However, with hard economic times around the world, more companies are realising that launching cheaper brands could boost global growth, and this trend is likely to accelerate in the future.

Product adaptation does not always have to be based on one market (unless it is a large one). There are bound to be similarities among similar market segments in, say, Brazil, Uruguay and Chile. Companies are therefore trying to adapt as much as possible on a regional basis to avoid losing economies of scale. Some successful companies have now adopted an approach of being as regional as possible and as local as necessary, cleverly building on the old cliché of "think global, act local".

Although it is possible to launch and sell regionally adapted products and still position them as international ones, advertising in most emerging markets is still predominantly local. Numerous studies have shown that dubbed advertising is culturally insensitive and irritates local pride. In many countries companies are even localising at a provincial level, taking into account cultural differences between different regions. It is also important to keep in mind an aspect of culture often ignored by western companies. Because most multinationals are at home in individualistic environments, they forget that other societies may value collective achievements more than individual ones. In Asia, for example, collectivism reigns and this has major implications for the advertising approach.

It goes without saying that packaging has to have local language on it, although some companies ignore this basic cultural adaptation. Even package sizes need to be different in certain markets; for example, consumer goods companies package detergents in smaller packs in poorer markets, and some sell tiny packages of cosmetics in very poor parts of Asia or Africa. This may put pressure on margins, but many companies feel it is necessary to capture that market segment. In some countries the focus is on selling larger packs at discount prices. In countries like Turkey, for instance, where there are frequent currency crises, buying big packs is a way for consumers to "hedge" the currency.

Understanding the local competition is crucial to success. "It is a nice fight between international competitors," says one experienced senior manager, "but the locals are formidable." Many large multinationals simply ignore domestic competition in their market entry or market expansion planning. This ignorance is based on arrogance and a feeling of superiority. It is a big mistake to think that domestic competitors will be easy to deal with. They may be protected by the government; they may produce more cheaply; they may be financed by capital that had previously been invested overseas; they are often willing to pay bribes to win deals; or they may be simply happy with lower profit margins. Domestic companies can be sophisticated and well run. Many also poach western executives, quickly learn from sophisticated foreign companies and are skilled copycats.

One of the side effects of tough domestic competition is something often not anticipated by multinationals: price wars. These have destroyed a number of otherwise good business plans, particularly for latecomers to the market. The stronger the market position, the easier it is to survive lower prices. Coming late to a market can increase this kind of price-related vulnerability.

8 Reaching the local market

We found that making the product available to every potential customer – and controlling that process well – has transformed our fortunes in developing countries.

Senior manager, fast-moving consumer goods company

Poor distribution networks and difficulties in making products available locally are major factors in the lack of success of many companies in emerging markets. This chapter looks at distribution: where companies most commonly run into problems and what they can do about them. Making products widely available is a daunting challenge in most emerging markets. Distribution networks are often fragmented, inefficient and full of potentially bankrupt partners. The rewards are rich for those who get it right, and huge sums are lost by those who get it wrong.

To get it right, several important principles should be followed.

Working with a distributor

Select the distributor carefully

Typically, there will be no shortage of companies wanting to distribute your products, but the selection process should be careful and thorough, involving a long list of important steps. These include:

- interviewing potential candidates;
- visiting their premises;
- checking their financial background with banks and credit-rating agencies (keeping in mind that this is no real guarantee);
- testing their technical expertise in sales and marketing;
- checking word-of-mouth recommendations;
- talking to retailers and end-buyers about them;
- checking the background of their relationship with retailers and end-buyers;
- checking their ability to provide customer and after-sales service;
- checking their nationwide reach.

The more information you get, the easier it should become to pick the right partner.

Ensure as much control as possible over the distribution network
This is best achieved by having a local office or staff on the ground who work closely with the distributor. Attempting to control things from a distance does not work. Some companies take full control and handle distribution themselves, using their own fleet of vehicles. Others place their own staff within the distributor's organisation, which offers advantages if run well. Another option is to include a "key person clause" in the distributor contract, guaranteeing that one of the distributor's staff will deal exclusively with your company on a daily basis. This can be costly for the distributor, and it can make sense and increase the sense of control to co-finance the salary of such a person.

Communicate clear goals to the local distributor

Distributors are often in business to make a quick profit and are not always concerned with the broader goals of proper brand building, the appropriate pricing strategy or the continuous maintenance of brand and product values. They may jump from distributing TV sets one day to detergents the next. But local distributors should know what your long-term strategic goals are. If they see they have a lucrative future by distributing your products, they may adapt their behaviour to suit your longer-term strategic business goals.

Never let the distributor define and build your brand

A distributor's suggestions may be clever and useful, but it is your company, ideally through your local organisation, that has to take care of marketing and brand positioning and building. Any marketing done by a distributor must be fully in tune with your overall marketing message. Remember also that distributors are often reluctant to distribute goods that require too much "push" (requiring extensive salesforce activity, for example). They prefer to work with companies that have invested in "pull" strategies (increasing consumer demand through, for example, advertising and other brand-building activities). Concerted and continuous brand building will help find and retain the best distributors and drive the business up.

Control pricing carefully

Pricing is a frequent cause of disputes. In emerging markets, a problem can be that resellers seek to sell products at a higher price than the company believes is appropriate for the market. Combating this is time- and resource-consuming, even when you have a strong local sales and marketing organisation. Possibly the best strategy to avoid pricing problems is to make the public aware what the price benchmark is through advertising. If people know what the price should be, they will try to avoid sellers who attempt to charge more. Colgate advised consumers to come directly to the company if they were unable to buy the product at the recommended price.

Keep distributors under pressure to improve performance

It is important to keep distributors on their toes and focused on ways to deliver. This can be done through short-term contracts, setting sales targets and then requiring strict and frequent reporting. Distributors must not become complacent and take your business for granted.

Provide training for distributors

Training helps to integrate a distributor's organisation and staff into your own. Technical and product update training is essential, but it is important to look at other areas where distributors have weaknesses (typically financial reporting and control, and often marketing and sales). Companies sometimes ask distributors to pay or co-pay for such training sessions; companies should pay for training themselves, however, if they see their partner is keen but financially weak. The danger is that trained individuals will leave and take their skills to other companies, but on balance it is a risk worth taking. Some companies insist that distributors keep newly trained individuals in certain posts and sometimes offer slightly better terms if people are kept in the post for which they were trained for a certain period of time.

Develop strong personal relationships with the distributor

To develop a constructive and productive relationship with a distributor, local presence is a prerequisite. The ultimate goal should be the creation of a sense of genuine partnership: a win-win relationship. This is not something that any company, regardless of its status and skills, can achieve overnight. It inevitably takes enormous amounts of time and energy, but it is worth building up both the tangible and intangible benefits of a commercial and personal relationship.

Managing the risk

Manage your receivables

Managing receivables is even more essential in emerging markets than it is in developed markets, but rigidly sticking to terms that require pre-payment in hard currency can stunt business development, especially once competition heats up and in markets where credit lines are tight and expensive. Successful emerging-markets players relax credit terms as trust develops, using their own research and experience to determine when and to whom to extend credit. But in volatile countries where the risk of crisis is high (especially a risk of banking system or currency collapse), it is sensible to be extra cautious. Only an experienced local team's closeness to the customer and market enables the appropriate balance to be struck on the basis of knowledge, trust and instinct. To diversify risk, many companies like to work with several distributors. If one collapses, at least not all of their outstanding receivables go with it. Despite the precautions, all companies will experience losses at some time and somewhere in the distribution channel, so they should have provisions and buffers in the budget in case money is lost. Many companies, for example Oracle, now prudently book income only when the money they are owed is safely in their bank account.

The risk sometimes lies not with the distributor but the distributors' bank. During economic crises, bank collapses increase. It is essential to have people monitoring the stability of the banking system, in particular the banks through which distributors work. Millions of dollars of outstanding payments can be stuck in a collapsed bank, resulting in serious losses for those who have left themselves exposed to such a risk. This is why many companies work with several banks to diversify the risk if one or two banks collapse.

Be ready to support distributors

This is particularly important if distributors do not have access to domestic or international loans. The cost of capital is high in most emerging economies and to establish and run a successful business, companies need to provide assistance to local partners. This can range from co-funded promotions involving anything from advertisements to trade fairs to help in securing credit lines. Most companies are reluctant to finance their distributor. Those that do see it as a necessary and temporary measure aimed at building the business. Others simply take their local distributor to their bank and say: "Give this guy a loan. We trust him. He will be working with us for many years to come."

Make sure the contract is sufficiently detailed

The following are some of the items that a contract with a distributor should contain:

- ◪ duration of the contract (limited to maintain pressure on performance);
- ◪ prices;
- ◪ terms and conditions of sales;
- ◪ rights to visit distributors' premises and inspect the accounts;
- ◪ protection against delivery delays (for example, if a product gets held up at a border);
- ◪ marketing and facilities expenditure;
- ◪ a cancellation clause (what constitutes a breach of the contract and how it will be dealt with);
- ◪ an agreed place for arbitration.

Some companies include buyback agreements in the contract, giving them control of inventories in case of devaluation. Remember that judicial systems even in developed emerging markets are overburdened, slow and often corrupt. Many companies insist that arbitration abroad is the only way to resolve commercial disputes.

Important things to remember

Be flexible and adapt to local circumstances

In emerging markets it is important to be creative in the way you approach things. If there are no distributors that have national reach, for example, why not invest in your own fleet of vans where drivers not only physically distribute but also take cash from small retailers. Many consumer goods companies have used this approach successfully. Although it appears expensive, the returns on such an investment have been good. If there is a problem with finding a good distributor on the ground, why not ask a distributor from a developed country to set up a distributorship for you? Ford did this in Bulgaria and became a market leader.

Caterpillar is another company famous for relying on its strong global dealer network to grow its business. However, because it could not find suitable dealers in Russia, it decided to handle distribution itself until suitable partners were found. An alternative is to buy a distributor and oversee and guide its operations. You cannot afford to let your business be dependent on incompetent or financially weak distributors. Hesitation in such matters gives competitors the opportunity to thrive and dominate. You do not necessarily need to remain in charge of distribution, but you must take steps to make sure that you have efficient distribution.

Emerging-market offices should regularly talk to each other and share knowledge. An approach tested in one country, such as sharing warehouse space with other companies or setting up supplier alliances, might offer useful lessons to other offices.

Consider combining several options to cover all market opportunities
Some IT companies, and no doubt others, sell their products and services through multiple channels. They sell directly to customers, to distributors, directly to dealers and through a select group of agents covering different areas of the market. This can be complicated, but if the set-up avoids overlap and it is clear who targets whom it can work well. If your distributor does a good job but cannot reach all customers, add more distributors in areas beyond your distributor's reach. Many companies prefer to keep this option open and therefore do not enter into exclusive contracts with distributors.

Handle key accounts yourself
These customers are too important to be left to distributors.

Don't ignore the rural customer
Forgetting about rural consumers can be a big mistake. In India, for example, Coca-Cola initially ignored the 750m-person rural market and focused on cities. As a result, the company (unusually) lagged behind Pepsi in terms of market share. Now, in an effort to crack the market, Coca-Cola has, among other things, bought a large chunk of domestic refrigerator production at a huge discount, which it passed on to small retailers in remote villages.

Consider franchising or flagship stores
Franchising or flagship stores are strategies that tend to work for such sectors as food, clothing or cosmetics. Franchising allows producers to create a retailing concept without jeopardising the product's image, which can be preserved through the careful choice of premium locations, employees, interior design and merchandising displays. One of the problems in getting the franchising concept up and running in many emerging markets is that local banks are unwilling to finance local franchising partners. Another common problem is that the franchising concept is not fully understood by local entrepreneurs. Franchisers must communicate relentlessly what the concept is and how it should be executed. They should make sure that contracts spell everything out in detail and that there is a clear exit strategy should things not work out.

Setting up your own shops to penetrate the market gives you control over all aspects of the business: the state of facilities, behaviour of staff, point of sale promotion and merchandising. The downside compared with franchising is cost, but flagship stores are often profitable ventures and good brand builders.

Keep a close eye on global retailers

As international retailers move into emerging markets, the distribution landscape changes dramatically. For a transition period, large consumer goods companies usually benefit from losing the middleman, but once retailers start getting entrenched the price squeeze starts. Companies have to be on top of the game and adapt as the rules change.

9 Manufacturing in emerging markets

We will keep moving our manufacturing to cheaper locations.

Gerard Kleisterlee, CEO, Philips

This chapter looks at why companies decide to relocate their manufacturing operations to cheaper locations and how they do it. It also outlines the many different types of tax and other incentives that companies can negotiate for when setting up manufacturing sites in emerging markets.

The manager of a large French multinational says:

> The only reason why we still manufacture our goods in France is because our CEO, who is French, does not want to be seen as someone who destroys French jobs. But I don't know how long we can maintain profitability medium term. Most of our competitors have already set up manufacturing in cheaper locations.

The French company's dilemma demonstrates that, on the one hand, global competitive pressures are forcing companies to lower their manufacturing cost while, on the other hand, there are emotional pressures pushing in the opposite direction. Furthermore, labour laws in western Europe make it expensive to shut down manufacturing facilities. Many senior managers have private reasons for wanting to stay put, and may justify the status quo by claiming that manufacturing in emerging markets is risky. But how risky is it really?

Companies that have many manufacturing facilities in emerging markets claim that the benefits far outweigh the risks and frustrations, provided the location is selected carefully and that entry into the market has been thoroughly prepared. Some aspects of manufacturing in emerging markets are complicated, but most of the worries people have are unjustified or exaggerated.

Take product quality, for example. Many of those who have set up manufacturing operations in emerging markets such as central and eastern Europe claim that the quality of output exceeds that achieved in Germany, Italy or the UK. Productivity may be lower, but this is offset by lower labour costs. In any case, published productivity figures mean nothing for an individual undertaking as they cover the whole country and include public and state-owned enterprises. If a multinational trains its own people to use its technology and implements top-notch manufacturing processes, it will quickly reach internal productivity benchmarks and far surpass national productivity levels.

For many emerging markets, the commercial evidence is clear: it pays to manufacture there and it is possible to manufacture good-quality products far more cheaply. For example, a large Japanese consumer electronics company says that manufacturing costs in emerging markets it has operations in are 35–40% lower than in developed markets.

The growth in free-trade agreements and the reduction in trade barriers around the world have made it viable to set up manufacturing operations in all kinds of places. For example, a growing number of Japanese companies now manufacture for the EU market in central and eastern Europe. But companies need to be careful about realities of free-trade agreements when making decisions about locating manufacturing operations. Many of the agreements simply do not work in practice as they are supposed to in theory.

There is no doubt that more manufacturing from the developed world will be transferred to emerging markets. The question is how quickly this will happen and where the investment will go. Will it be concentrated in a few "stars" or will it be more widespread? Will it continue to shift to even cheaper locations as labour costs rise?

Many multinationals are in the process of rethinking their global manufacturing strategies. They want to reduce the number of manufacturing sites globally to a minimum. If most of the world is going to become a large free-trade area, they say, then unless, say, transport costs would be prohibitive (as they would for a cement manufacturer), it makes sense to make a product in as few locations as possible. By benefiting massively from economies of scale, the plants will significantly reduce cost per unit. This is probably the next big global manufacturing trend, and it is likely to accelerate as trade becomes genuinely freer. At the same time, it has huge implications for governments in emerging markets.

This shift of manufacturing to cheaper locations is inevitable and irreversible. The developed world has already seen a shift from agricultural to industrial societies, and now services are driving economies. As the GDP of developed-world economies shifts to services, industrial manufacturing shifts to the developing world.

Once a decision has been made to leave a developed-world manufacturing location for a cheaper one, two things dominate the next steps:

choosing a location and deciding how to make the investment (for example, through a joint venture or acquisition; see Chapter 10).

Choosing a location

The process for selecting a manufacturing location involves:

◪ determining project criteria (see below), assumptions and requirements;
◪ producing a list of potential locations;
◪ analysing in detail each location according to your criteria;
◪ producing a shortlist of locations and evaluating them further by, for example, interviewing real-estate agents and construction companies, assessing the availability of suppliers, assessing other companies manufacturing there, evaluating infrastructure development plans, validating desk research findings, discussing incentives at different government levels;
◪ visiting sites, interviewing and starting negotiations.

About 150 countries are considered to be developing countries. Some are not suitable for manufacturing, lacking such basic infrastructure as reliable power supplies and having too few sufficiently skilled workers. Some are in the middle of an armed conflict and security issues would be overwhelming. Others have disadvantages such as trading arrangements that will hinder exports. But there are many excellent, inexpensive places around the world in which to locate manufacturing operations.

Criteria for choosing a manufacturing location

◪ Which firms have set up operations and what are their experiences?
◪ What is the ease and cost of shipment to desired export locations, and how good is the transport infrastructure?
◪ Are there signed free-trade agreements? Do they work in practice? What other agreements are being negotiated?
◪ Which suppliers (domestic and foreign) operate in the country? How good are they? What are their experiences? Will your existing suppliers support you if you switch to this location?
◪ What investment incentives will be available?
◪ How easy will it be to set up operations and run them from day to day?

- What are labour costs likely to be? What is the availability of both skilled and unskilled local workers? What is the unemployment level in the region and the country as a whole?
- How easy will it be to obtain land and other permits?
- Will it be possible to operate seven days a week, 24 hours a day in flexible shifts?
- What is the strength and attitude of trade unions? Will you be able to hire workers on individual contracts? Will you have the flexibility to hire and fire workers according to demand?
- Are there any special economic zones with tax and customs benefits?
- Will it be possible to get cheap or free land and reduced prices for services such as electricity and water?

Incentives and privileges

Companies are naturally coy about the importance of investment incentives. Interview a manager on the record and the last thing he will say is that investment was heavily influenced by investment incentives. Talk to the same person off the record and he will smile and say: "Why would I put the money in a country with no tax holidays, if all other criteria are similar? Would you?"

Multinationals are often unaware of how many privileges they can extract from governments. Many incentives are not immediately apparent in the law. In reality, many deals are made in meetings with officials and many firms now negotiate investment incentives beyond what the law appears to allow for. One senior director of a well-known European multinational said its strategy regarding investment incentives was simple: "Apply, complain, negotiate, and if it does not work move to a new country where it will." Of course, many countries offer packages and special economic zones that are sufficiently attractive without the need for tough negotiations.

What do multinationals want – and get – from many governments?

- Tax breaks of 10–15 years (usually conveniently counting from the first year of profit). Needless to say, creative transfer pricing (the prices at which subsidiaries of the same firm move goods across national boundaries), for example, can delay that first profitable year for quite some time. (For example, a multinational company with operations in an emerging market buys some goods or services from its own plants elsewhere. These are often overcharged to the emerging-market operation and thus reduce the profit and delay tax payments to the host country.

◾ Duty-free import of any machinery (including any VAT exemptions).
◾ Tax or other incentives at regional or provincial level (including any local tax breaks).
◾ Free or cheap land.
◾ Free or cheap connections to water and electricity supplies and subsidised running costs.
◾ Necessary infrastructure around the factory. Japan's Matsushita, for example, persuaded local authorities in the Czech Republic to build a road from the factory to the main road.
◾ A brownfield site (an empty, abandoned building, which can be used either immediately or after some refurbishment).
◾ Employment grants for each created job (some countries offer €5,000–10,000 per person).

Companies should not base their investment decision solely on the investment incentives they are offered or can negotiate. The decision should be made taking all the important criteria into account. But if you have shortlisted several locations with similar advantages, then why not go "tax shopping", focusing on both national and local authorities.

China's erogenous zones

China currently attracts $50 billion in foreign direct investment a year – around 25% of all investment headed for emerging markets – and the amount is increasing. A huge domestic market, low labour costs and a fast-developing network of excellent local suppliers make up a large part of the equation; the remainder is incentives. Most investors still go to 50 special economic zones (some just at city level). As well as zones, cities have the authority to offer special deals with land and utility prices. The benefits for the country are clear. Economic growth averaged 8% between 1996 and 2003, and exports grew from $50 billion in 1990 to $410 billion in 2003. The future for China seems bright.

The negotiating position of governments has been weakening as the competition to attract foreign direct investment has grown stronger.

Between 1998 and 2001, foreign direct investment (FDI) to emerging markets was $200 billion–250 billion a year. Now it is stuck at the lower end of that range. Investors are now likely to say: "If you don't want to give us this incentive, there are countries that will be happy to do so."

It is hard for a government, looking at a high unemployment rate and a vulnerable current account, to say no. The multiplier effect of one large multinational manufacturing facility is powerful, bringing in more investors (as suppliers) and boosting the local supplier and servicing industry. This is why governments are willing to give incentives to powerful multinationals to invest in their countries. Success feeds on success. Economically, the impact of FDI on developing economies is enormous. In Poland, for example, the top five regions (coincidentally those that attracted the largest amount of FDI) have grown eight times faster than the bottom five (that had virtually none) since the beginning of the economic transition from communism. Differences in unemployment in such regions are enormous, ranging from 5–6% in the most developed regions to over 30% in the least developed ones.

Many governments do not truly understand the way in which big foreign investors decide where to manufacture. Companies like IBM hold sessions with government officials to explain how multinational companies make investment decisions. This helps create greater understanding between a company and a government and is likely to result in proposals that work for both. Governments that still feel they are in a position to bring in new investors without incentives are likely to find that their economic growth is slower than that of countries that provide incentives to attract foreign firms. Russia, for example, has attracted only a fraction of China's investment, despite its large market and low labour costs. This is partly because the federal government does not offer incentives for foreign investors, and its attitude to them is, at best, lukewarm. Negative perceptions of the market among senior managers have not helped (see Chapter 17).

Manufacturing operations in some emerging markets have suffered from adverse publicity in recent years, mainly on the grounds of working conditions, the use of child labour and environmental issues. It is crucial that companies operating in emerging markets are socially responsible (see Chapter 13), whether they run things themselves or outsource to subcontractors.

Subcontracting is increasing in certain industries. A number of pharmaceuticals companies use high-tech Turkish companies to manufacture their products while they focus on marketing and sales. Good subcontractors are not easy to find in emerging markets. They also need to be supervised, monitored and controlled in order to avoid bad publicity for the company that uses them.

10 Making acquisitions work

Buying multibillion-dollar companies in the United States is a breeze compared to buying small companies in emerging markets.

Senior director, Kraft Foods

Everything is worth only what a purchaser is willing to pay for it.

Publius, 1BC

This chapter looks at the important lessons of acquisitions and joint ventures in emerging markets and considers what successful companies have done to avoid acquisitions and joint ventures going wrong.

Buying companies in emerging markets is like walking through a minefield. But, surprisingly, many companies start rambling through it without a mine detector. Acquisitions often fail in the developed world, as numerous studies have shown, but in emerging markets everything is much more complicated and the success rate is often low or at best mixed.

For a company to survive it has to grow, and it has to be stronger than its competitors. This presents a company with a strategic choice. Should it rely on organic growth, investing in and developing existing businesses and launching new businesses? The process is slower but the risks are lower. Or should it grow by acquisition, buying other businesses? Growth is rapid but the risks are higher. Companies need to evaluate whether an acquisition is more cost-effective than organic growth for achieving a desired market position. It should offer clear advantages over achieving the same objectives through organic growth. Many companies feel that if there is no brand name, market share or strategic competitive advantage to purchase, then it is probably much better not to be exposed to an acquisition minefield.

Acquiring companies in emerging markets is complex, and it is dangerous to underestimate this. Most companies make mistakes in the acquisition process, with poor due diligence before the purchase or poor management during post-acquisition restructuring. Some mistakes cause almost irreparable damage to the business; others are less lethal but cause disruptions, delays and temporarily disappointing results.

A decision on whether an acquisition is the right way to go and at what price should be based on comparing the two options. First, determine the cost of setting up a new operation and achieving new sales from scratch. Second, look at the cost of making an acquisition and any post-acquisition restructuring. These estimates are not easy to make.

Types of acquisitions

◪ Vertical acquisitions: the acquired company is either a customer or a supplier of the acquirer.

◪ Horizontal acquisitions: an acquirer buys companies in the same industry to achieve better market position and gain economies of scale.

◪ Concentric acquisitions: an acquirer buys additional product lines or technologies to share resources (for higher profitability).

◪ Conglomerate acquisitions: an acquirer expands the total portfolio of businesses.

Source: Rock, M.L., Rock, R.H. and Sikora, H., *The Mergers and Acquisitions Handbook*, 2nd edition, McGraw Hill, 1994, p. 5

When considering an acquisition strategy in emerging markets, companies should ask several fundamental questions.

◪ Do we, as a company and a group of individuals, know how to acquire successfully, especially in emerging markets?

◪ Do we have dedicated internal resources (time, knowledgeable people, money) to seek out and engage in cross-border acquisitions?

◪ Are we aware that there may be potential problems with acquisitions in the market we are looking at?

◪ Are we aware that we need to spend significant time and money to identify potential problems before making a purchasing decision?

◪ Are we aware that our usual investment bankers may not be the best advisers, especially if they do not have a long-standing local presence in the market under consideration, and that we should consider working with well-informed locally based (domestic or international) advisers?

◪ Are the managers we value most and most want to retain for or against acquiring? This is important because internal resistance may undermine an acquisition.

In emerging markets the goal of acquisition is often geographic expansion as well as strategically limiting the manoeuvring space of key international and domestic competitors. Whatever the aim, in emerging markets it is essential to be vigorous in seeking out opportunities and taking advantage of them. There are not many great acquisition targets in individual emerging markets and the competition to buy them can be fierce. It is often the fast firms that buy companies, not the big ones, so you need to identify and approach the best targets early. It is best to have a dedicated acquisition team or teams, which can give you a competitive advantage. Assigning a manager with other duties to lead acquisitions often results in a lack of necessary speed and dedication. Needless to say, local presence is a great help.

Having a constant eye open for targets pays, especially in countries where governments sell their state holdings through quickly announced tenders. Deadlines for submitting bids can be short, leaving little time to conduct due diligence properly. Being on top of developments and fostering good relationships with governments and managers of target companies will increase the chances of submitting a bid on time (without plunging into the unknown). Worthwhile acquisition targets in emerging markets are those that hold good market shares and good brands, and whose processes and earnings can further be improved with better management skills and focus and/or injections of new capital investment. Most acquisition targets in emerging markets need thorough restructuring and, in particular, the introduction of more efficient management systems. This is both an opportunity and a threat, and should be approached in that fashion.

Companies should avoid looking at just one country. Regional or global acquisition teams should have an overview of several countries within particular trading blocs (where exporting does not encounter obstacles) in order to be able to spot opportunities quickly.

Experience in the developed world has shown that acquisitions within the same industry often offer the best chances for success. Diversification through acquisition can be an effective strategy, but is a risky one to pursue in more challenging markets. Synergies typically play a crucial role. A company that acquires a firm in a familiar industry can use its experience and expertise to integrate it into its worldwide operations. Lack of familiarity with the industry can prevent the successful integration of the target company's operations with those of the acquiring company.

After a company decides that it wants to acquire, rather than grow organically, it should:

◪ establish acquisition criteria;
◪ identify candidates;
◪ perform due diligence and valuation;
◪ negotiate the purchase;
◪ restructure and integrate.

Establishing acquisition criteria

Once a company decides it has the capability to make acquisitions and run the acquired business successfully, it should determine its acquisition criteria and, more importantly, keep them in mind. Too often companies pay much more than they wanted to. After all the work that has gone into the process, the thinking is that an additional 10–20% will not kill them. Moreover, acquisition teams become so close to the potential transaction that they are willing to overlook certain criteria. The project has become "their baby" and they do not want to see it fail. Some managers decide on acquisitions because of their own private interest and the money they can make. It is therefore not surprising that much research on the success of acquisitions shows that they often fail to bring value to shareholders.

The criteria should describe the ideal candidate and can be used as a benchmark against which to measure acquisition candidates. It should start with external criteria that cover the political, economic and business environment. These are covered in more detail in the checklists in previous chapters, but they should address the following kinds of questions.

◪ Political situation: what is the political risk we will be willing to live with?
◪ Economic situation: what is the economic risk or economic situation we will be willing to live with?
◪ Government regulations: will the government enable us to compete fairly and without interference?
◪ Trade constraints: can we rely on the free-trade agreements that are in place?
◪ Infrastructure: will it be possible to ship goods out of the country efficiently and at minimum cost?

Internal criteria, focusing on the acquisition target, should focus on tangible and measurable benefits. Below is a selection, but each company must create its own list based on its specific needs.

- Market share: what is it now and what position would we like to capture?
- Existence and method of distribution: how much should the distribution network be developed?
- Price: how much money can we spend on an acquisition?
- Cost of labour: what is the maximum cost of labour we will be willing to accept?
- Strengths: what competitive strengths would we consider attractive in an acquisition target?
- Weaknesses: what weaknesses of an acquisition target will we be willing to correct? What weaknesses will stop us from acquiring?
- Quality: does the product have to be of exportable quality?
- Trade unions: how strong are they and are we prepared to work with them?

Identifying acquisition candidates

Identifying acquisition candidates that meet the criteria is time-consuming and some aspects of the search are complex. It may be quite easy to find a list of all companies active in a certain industry and to analyse external criteria, but it is difficult to get to grips with the internal position of potential candidates. Financial statements, in general, cannot be taken at face value, and recent accounting scandals in the developed world make people even more sceptical about the quality of financial information in emerging markets. To avoid unpleasant surprises, it is sensible to use many different sources to verify internal information, especially during the due diligence process.

Identifying the most attractive acquisition candidate in the developed world can involve looking at several hundred companies in order to identify the most attractive. Acquisition candidates are not nearly as numerous in emerging markets, except in a few large countries. Background research can provide an initial list of candidates in a specific industry. It is also quite easy to identify successful exporters, which gives a good indication of hard-currency earnings and the relative competitiveness of the goods they produce.

Far more difficult to find is relevant and accurate financial information, information about the domestic industry and any relevant competitive intelligence, without which you would never make an acquisition in the developed world. For some products, for example, it is virtually impossible to find reliable consumption data; and different sources often state substantially different numbers. To make things worse, domestic companies in emerging markets are often particularly secretive about their operations and most are not listed on stock exchanges. Even if they are, many stock exchanges in emerging markets are more loosely regulated than in the developed world and the quality of disclosure leaves a lot to be desired.

The process of identifying candidates has to be heavily based on direct contacts. It is the best and sometimes only way to find out enough about a potential acquisition target to start due diligence. Getting senior and other relevant managers or owners of potential candidate firms to co-operate is essential. Techniques for getting managers on your side include:

- promising them that they will keep their jobs and remain an integral part of the company (many companies promise to keep old managers as honorary presidents or consultants, often increasing their pay and giving them bigger offices, which makes them feel more important – but they do not give them any decision-making power);
- promising them higher incomes and a better future;
- taking them to corporate headquarters to explain strategy and impress them;
- taking them to see successful acquisitions in other countries.

All such actions are a great help in building mutual trust and understanding. These trust-building measures may become a decisive factor in the due diligence process in emerging markets. A local management that is supportive and gives clear signals of co-operation will make this process much more revealing, and therefore more effective.

Performing due diligence and valuation

The due diligence process involves intensive fact-finding about and thorough analysis of an acquisition target. All due diligence actions aim to answer three critical questions.

- Is the target really as attractive as it appears on the surface?
- Will it fit well into our sales and profit growth plans?

◪ Can it be restructured and managed in a way that will help us profitably grow the business?

A large amount of information needs to be processed and understood to answer these questions.

Performing thorough due diligence is crucial for the success of any acquisition in emerging markets. This may seem obvious, but as in the developed world, it is surprising how many companies carry out half-hearted due diligence, sometimes even after the deal has been done "to verify what was bought". No wonder surveys reveal that a majority of acquisitions fail to meet set objectives and do not create shareholder value.

A plan for how the due diligence is to be conducted should cover the following.

◪ **Who will do the job?** Who will be the members of the team and outside researchers/consultants, and how will they communicate with each other? Who will be responsible for which due diligence activities? Always make sure that senior management is closely involved. It may be tempting to let a management consultancy and/or an investment bank take the lead, but this is an easy way to lose the feel for the deal. Most due diligence processes leave unanswered questions, and the proportion of "unknown" at the end of the process is much larger in emerging markets. So inevitably a large part of the final decision has to be based on the feel – a qualitative characteristic. If senior managers are detached from an investigation and lack first-hand contact with the deal, it will diminish the company's ability to make a sound purchasing decision.

◪ **Sources of information.** What approach will be used for the investigation? Which sources will be used? Are these all the sources that can be used, or are there other excellent sources that you do not know about? To get the most objective picture of the candidate, talk to customers, distributors, industry experts, think-tanks, suppliers, trade unions, management, workers and competitors.

◪ **Key information.** Which information is the most crucial for making the decision? Is it possible to find multiple sources to verify this information? Which information is merely "nice to know"? Do not waste time and resources on this type of information, but if it is easy to get, then get it to give a more complete picture. Remember that the quality of information is more important than the quantity.

There are general checklists of information necessary for any due diligence process, but each acquisition requires its own specific checklist too. The list of specifics to investigate in emerging markets is particularly long, and many items are notoriously hard to investigate and understand. Although in theory all information should be analysed in depth, in practice this is hard to achieve in emerging markets. Lawyers and investment bankers claim that companies rarely feel they understand as much as they would expect, based on their experience in the developed world. This can be discouraging, but companies should still aim for the most in-depth investigations possible. This will enable them to evaluate the strengths and weaknesses of the target in respect of existing and potential competitors and give them confidence to proceed with the acquisition. Most importantly, a view will emerge on what the potential earnings may be and, ultimately, on how much to pay.

A target evaluation typically comprises the following broad areas:

- strategy and background;
- markets, products and marketing;
- distribution and sales;
- financial audit;
- manufacturing and technology;
- environmental audit;
- legal audit;
- organisational structure and human resources.

Companies should also supplement the above with a thorough understanding of the checklist in Chapter 3.

Strategy and background
This part of the evaluation should focus on describing the acquisition target in the past and the present, as well as its strategy. It is important to know the company's strategic strengths and weaknesses.

Markets, products and marketing
A buyer obviously needs an in-depth understanding of the business's products (or services). It is also crucial to determine the market share potential of the business's products, particularly when buying market

share is the primary motive for the acquisition. In doing this, market developments and trends should be taken into account.

Here is a selection of important questions a buyer should answer.

- ◪ What is the product portfolio and what are its market shares? How have market shares moved up or down in the past and why? What are the USPS (unique selling propositions), pricing history and profit margins? What will drive demand for products and their prices in the future? What is the risk of price wars?
- ◪ What is the product positioning? How is it perceived by customers and how has it influenced sales levels in various market segments?
- ◪ How do competitors, distributors and consumers perceive the product and its quality? Conduct primary research and detect any dissatisfaction and negative brand perceptions early.
- ◪ If we would improve the quality and service of the product(s), would that have a positive impact on potential earnings?
- ◪ How has the market segment in general behaved in the past and what is driving demand? Is this market segment under pressure or shrinking relative to other segments? Is it cyclical and how long are the cycles? Which market segments are actually growing?
- ◪ Will we need to upgrade quality and how expensive will that be?
- ◪ Can we and should we use that facility to develop and manufacture new products for various market segments that are growing?
- ◪ How large should marketing and advertising expenses be to accelerate demand and earnings in the future?
- ◪ Is the domestic industry in question profitable? What have the profitability cycles been in the past and what are they likely to be in the future?
- ◪ Are there any complex measures in the customs system of the target country that will inhibit imports or exports?

Distribution and sales

Efficient distribution is a key competitive advantage in complex and rapidly changing emerging markets. Distribution networks are grossly underdeveloped in virtually all emerging markets. Although many are developing fast, it can take years if not decades for them to match those that are found in the developed world. Therefore it often makes sense for companies to acquire an enterprise that has a distribution network in place.

Even if it does not have warehousing facilities and a fleet of vehicles, an acquisition target should have in-depth knowledge of the distribution system and the options and methods open to it and used by its competitors. It should also have a pool of sales people who are familiar with local distribution problems and have good contacts with customers.

Financial audit

Financial projections should be based on careful analysis of what assumptions are sound and of the drivers of demand. The key is to look for future earnings potential. Before any financial projections are created, all the due diligence issues should be examined. When examining the business's financial statements, buyers should keep in mind that these are frequently ambiguous and unreliable and that accounting standards often differ from international norms. Buyers should make their own assumptions about the expected future earnings performance and cash flows from an acquisition rather than rely on what the seller tells them.

Ultimately, the financial audit should determine the value of the business, but there are almost always disagreements between buyer and seller concerning the realistic value of the company. Past performance is not a useful indicator for business valuation in emerging markets, so buyers try to make price a function of the business's earnings potential. Sellers rarely agree with this valuation approach and often put high values on past sales and, often stretching credibility, on their fixed assets.

Price is not necessarily the principal issue in reaching agreement on an acquisition. Treatment of management and workers often plays an important role, as do promises of further investments and on-the-job training programmes, particularly in countries that were formerly communist.

Determining market value is not easy for a number of reasons.

- ◪ **Lack of reliable information.** Many companies are not listed so valuing them is similar to valuing a closely held business in the developed world. There is often no central authority that can provide any meaningful information on the company's standing. Even if it is listed, not all exchanges are well regulated. Attempts to compare a company with others are equally problematic. In many emerging markets, it is difficult to obtain financial statements.

◪ **Irrelevant past earnings.** Earnings forecasts should be crucial in value determination. But getting a true past financial picture on which to base forecasts is tricky. Past earnings are distorted by the lack of competitive market conditions, especially in countries with a communist legacy. Larger state enterprises are often sole producers or virtual monopolies as a result of government protectionism. After privatisation, barriers to entry and good government connections fall by the wayside. The implications for future cash flows are enormous. It is essential to investigate how much the company's earnings may be boosted by monopoly privileges, low-interest loans, privileged access to government contracts, subsidised rents or other government help. By removing these factors from cash-flow calculations, a more realistic picture emerges, often turning a money-spinner into a potential money-loser. This sounds sensible, but how do you go about evaluating the cash-flow generating ability of companies that have never operated without subsidies or subtle government protection? All you can do is carry out due diligence and detailed analysis of the industry, trade trends, quality of products, competition and other fundamentals in order to fully understand the drivers of future sales.

Since official financial information is of limited value, it is important to tap managers at all levels and workers for accurate information about the state of an enterprise. They will be well acquainted with the problems of distribution and supplies, the state of machinery, and to some extent their customers and end-users. One investment banker maintains he can get more out of one meeting with an enterprise's production manager than many meetings with the general manager; this is something to keep in mind.

◪ **Overvalued assets.** Many buyers have found that balance sheets reveal little useful information. The problem is that assets, especially equipment, are often overvalued in a firm's official financial statements. In many countries, assets also often have longer lives and lower depreciation rates than in the developed world. You may find that certain assets have never been depreciated. It is a particular problem in former communist countries, where central state funds were disbursed based on the size of assets. But assets are worth only what they are able to produce and this should be the basis for valuation. If they can only produce an outdated product poorly, they are worthless, a fact that local companies find hard to believe.

◪ **Accounts receivable and accounts payable.** It is crucial to check whether receivables listed are enforceable. In many countries the quality of the courts is poor and trying to enforce receivables through them is often impossible. In some countries it is useful to check whether the companies were allowed to or whether they have written off any doubtful receivables. Another option is to try to negotiate a purchase without taking over the receivables. Signed contracts promising new production orders are another potential trap. They should not be accepted at face value; investigation should be made into how likely they are to materialise. The system of inter-company invoicing and recording of receivables is slow and inefficient in some emerging markets. Unpaid invoices pile up and demands for payment become impossible to enforce.

◪ **Inter-enterprise debt.** Given tight credit conditions and high interest rates in many emerging markets, local companies have difficulties in obtaining bank loans. By using private connections, enterprises borrow from each other but some then default on payments. Extreme care should be taken during due diligence to try to determine the level of inter-enterprise debt. Many such debts are never recorded on a balance sheet. One company was hit by millions of dollars of old debt several months after a purchase in Bulgaria. Another component of inter-enterprise debt is inter-company borrowing. In some instances it is not only money that is owed. One firm was stunned when approached by a nearby company demanding 100 workers for a month. It had previously lent 100 workers to the acquired firm and now wanted the favour returned.

◪ **Tax and social security liabilities.** An important part of the financial audit is to check for any tax liabilities and for the impact of tax payments or non-payments on financial statements. Many firms have discovered that their acquisition targets had not paid tax or social security for years, thus creating a large potential liability and inflating their results. Some firms have been pursued by the tax authorities after the acquisition to pay the back tax. The risk of this happening should be avoided by thorough due diligence.

◪ **Politicisation.** Business valuation is not purely a financial issue. It often requires sensitivity to political issues, for example when buying a state-owned company or when local public opinion is hostile to foreign takeovers. Some firms have done "face-saving" deals with local governments and privatisation bodies, whereby a higher sale price is publicly announced and creative ways are found to convince the government to put some of the money back into the company after the transaction is completed.

As the number of acquisitions in emerging markets increases, multinationals are using market comparison values more and more. They increasingly use prices paid for previous acquisitions as yardsticks to enable them to come to a figure for the acquisition currently under consideration. Investment bankers generally compare acquisition deals by looking at an entire region because of similarities between countries and industries.

Companies whose senior management is supportive of long-term business development are sometimes prepared to pay well over current value. They are more concerned about what the purchase can bring in terms of long-term earnings streams and what it means strategically, if it captures, for example, an important local brand and so limits the competition's room for manoeuvre.

Nevertheless, a buyer should try to create a business plan based on future profit estimates, taking all the uncertainties involved into account, and measure it against the price being asked for the business.

The value of a candidate as a going concern depends on future cash flows and earnings, discounted back to the present using an appropriate discount rate. When trying to determine the appropriate discount rate, it is necessary to make adjustments for distortions created by monopolies, subsidies and past (perhaps now irrelevant) trading relationships. This is of course a subjective process, but some provisions should be made. Further problems arise when trying to make realistic assumptions on future performance. This is especially hard when trying to predict a target company's sales and profits in five years' time. Emerging markets can change rapidly for a number of reasons, such as the threat of economic crisis, changing consumer habits and new domestic or international competitors.

Manufacturing and technology
The main goal of this part of the investigation is to estimate the investment that will be required after acquisition to integrate the acquired

business into a global manufacturing system and to achieve desired standards of productivity and quality. An assessment should also be made to determine the ease and cost of expanding the facility for any future increases in demand.

The investigation should answer some of the following questions.

- What are the current manufacturing processes and the capacity and state of equipment? How productive is the facility?
- How are supply channels organised? What has been the behaviour of supply channel participants? What are the current supply problems?
- If there are any problems with the supply of components, can these be solved? What is the local supplier base of manufacturing components like? Will we have to persuade our global suppliers to invest nearby?
- What are the availability and prices of raw materials? How are those likely to behave in the next five years?
- Are there R&D facilities and researchers that could be integrated into the buyer's regional and global strategy?

Environmental audit

In some sectors, this audit should be the first due diligence step. Companies often find environmental damage on site. The audit should establish the extent of damage and, more importantly, indicate how the liability can be contractually avoided. Several companies have made acquisitions and have later been asked by local authorities to clean up the damage that was there before the purchase. Buyers should make it clear before the purchase that they will not be held responsible for any existing environmental damage.

Legal audit

A legal audit typically includes such things as the following.

- **Ownership structure.** It is sometimes tricky to find out who really owns a company. It does happen that firms negotiate for months with people who claim they own the business but in fact do not.
- **Restitution.** Restitution claims on property should be checked, especially in countries with a socialist legacy. If a claim comes after an acquisition, this can create serious problems. For

example, in Hungary one buyer could not raise local financing until the restitution claim was resolved, which took many months.

- ◪ **Corporate agreements.** Close examination of the various corporate agreements is important. For example, you may find that certain deals among shareholders shed a new light on management decisions and appointments, or sharing of profits.
- ◪ **Labour contracts.** A careful review of labour contracts is essential. For example, managers may be entitled to large payments upon termination of their employment and may receive huge bonuses regardless of the enterprise's performance.

Organisational structure and human resources

It is important to understand the existing management structure in order to change it successfully. Former communist countries had inefficient management structures. There was widespread overmanning, no sense of the concept of customer satisfaction and a reluctance among workers to take responsibility. The due diligence process must look at the costs and requirements of reorganisation, since without substantial reorganisation most acquisitions are doomed to fail.

It is also important to know who the important people in the organisation are, at both management and supervisory level. Will there be extra costs if these people are kept on? Are they likely to leave? What would keep them with the company? Acquisitions often fail because some key employees are unwilling to work with new employers and decide to leave. If a new structure and systems are imposed, will these be in sharp contrast to the existing systems in the target? If significant work has to be done, this will have to be planned for and executed during the post-acquisition restructuring.

Negotiating terms of purchase

After carrying out due diligence, the acquisition team usually has a reasonably good idea of what it would be willing to pay for a business. Buyers now need to be patient and persistent, because negotiations in emerging markets frequently take far longer than expected. In some cases, it can take more than a year to conduct due diligence thoroughly and as long again to negotiate a deal. In other cases, negotiations involve competing domestic parties, including various ministries or different governmental bodies. Or the target's management, favourable to an acquisition, may be forced by outside pressure to resign before a deal is concluded, sending negotiations back to square one.

Delays can create serious problems. The acquisition target may lose value after the bid is submitted and while negotiations are going on. When buyers lower their offer to reflect the change, government officials may insist that the previous bid is binding, thus lengthening negotiations for several more months. To avoid this problem, buyers should include a clause in the contract allowing the final price to be renegotiated in certain specified circumstances.

The power of lobby groups should not be underestimated during both due diligence and negotiations. Many deals are politically sensitive and governments are usually under pressure from the public not to sell their "family silver" too cheaply. It is worth spending time to find out how ministries and privatisation agencies are connected to the target enterprises; in many cases, the people in charge are "old buddies" or have some kind of connection through a seat on the supervisory board. If they receive a fee as a member of the supervisory board, they are generally not keen to do anything that could lead to a change in the status quo. One Coca-Cola manager who negotiated numerous deals in emerging countries argues that non-stop lobbying, political connections and persistence are some of the key skills needed to get through the negotiation process successfully. He says:

> You have to be networking all around, with all the key players, and all the time. This builds key relationships, which are critical if you want to get something done.

A well-judged accompanying public relations campaign is important. Many investors find all sorts of negative rumours circulating in the local press once their acquisition intentions become public or even, worryingly, before that. Most centre on how the company is planning to shut down the plant and dismiss most of the workers. This puts further pressure on the authorities and complicates the negotiation process.

The corporate communications division, with the help of an established locally based PR agency, should draw up a campaign to start as early as possible, even during the due diligence process. The goal is to pre-empt negative publicity by focusing on positive issues such as maintaining employment and promising a good future for the whole enterprise and the region. Donations to a local school or hospital will also help to gain acceptance in the local community (see Chapter 13).

Bad press usually originates from labour leaders in the target enterprise so it is crucial to identify and communicate with key workers (many enterprises have this on their due diligence checklists). A lack of employee support may not destroy negotiations, but it is now widely believed that gaining this support early during due diligence is good for fact-finding and for final negotiations. Getting the target's management on the buyer's side is also important. Not many governments are willing to do a deal if management and employees are not keen on the sale (especially in cases of sales of state property).

Eyes on the ball, ears to the ground

One of the challenges throughout a negotiation process is keeping track of where the deal is in the decision-making pipeline, and then maintaining contact with the appropriate officials and managers. This can only be done if there are people who can keep their ears to the ground and their eyes on how things are progressing. Important papers can get lost in bureaucratic channels or new competition can enter the market. These are not things that you find out about in good time without a local presence.

Before submitting a bid for a state-owned company, the investor needs to be aware of the government's goals. It is useful to know where the proceeds from a privatisation sell-off will go, as this can shape motivations. Some governments are interested in price, especially if the money will go directly into the budget. Others are looking for a buyer with a good track record of managing acquisitions while minimising lay-offs, and which has big investment plans or a strong emphasis on production for export. Since negotiations often extend over many months and conditions change, companies need to be alert to changes in government attitudes; for example, if unemployment starts to rise, a government may well start to pay more attention to the employment side of the negotiation.

Below is a list of some of the non-price evaluation criteria that will be in the minds of those selling government-owned companies.

- Willingness to provide employment guarantees for a certain period of time.
- Enhancement of the export earnings potential.
- Improvement of the technological standards.
- Readiness to reinvest profits.
- Readiness to use local suppliers or bring in other foreign suppliers as new investors.
- Immediate and future improvements of environmental standards.

◪ Guarantee of future investment plans.

◪ Taking over old debts (and lessening the pressure on the state budget).

How large a stake to buy?

If there is one clear principle in emerging markets it is: never buy a non-controlling stake in a domestic enterprise. Without control over the daily operations of the enterprise, all restructuring efforts are likely to be severely hampered. But, where political sensitivities or the size of the local company make buying a majority stake impossible, there are other ways to gain operational control. One is to have a majority of seats on the management board despite a minority or non-controlling stake. Needless to say this is hard to negotiate. Another is to use so-called management contracts, where the minority shareholder (buyer) is hired as manager for a specified period, usually until it can purchase a majority stake.

Sometimes companies buy minority stakes, but this is usually only the case when local companies are truly large and very strategic, such as large oil companies in Russia, or in countries where it may be legally impossible to buy a majority stake in all businesses or in those deemed strategic. The goal is to use the involvement in the company to learn more about the potential purchase of a majority stake and in the meantime earn some profits/dividends.

Restructuring and integration

Post-acquisition restructuring in emerging markets is costly and time-consuming. Integrating different working attitudes and cultures is always difficult, but most emerging-market businesses require a substantial overhaul if they are to become an integral and successful part of the buyer's company. This is why many companies investing in an emerging market opt for a greenfield investment.

One of the most complicated issues in post-acquisition restructuring is trying to increase productivity. This typically involves laying off many employees, so the first stage has to involve a positive public relations campaign and communication with opinion leaders among the workforce. If they turn against the deal after it is completed, the company can suffer immense difficulties. One large American multinational bought a local manufacturer and then struggled to make efficiency gains in the manufacturing process. After some investigation, the company learned that several foremen were ignoring any orders from above and telling workers to do things in the old way. When these individuals were identified they were not laid off. On the contrary, they were told they were doing a good job and were sent, with their families, for a year of intensive training in the United States. By the time they returned they had become champions of the corporate agenda and the need to increase productivity.

In many countries acquisition contracts stipulate no lay-offs for a certain period, usually ranging from one to three years. Multinationals may be opposed to such agreements, but many recognise that they are an important way of showing sensitivity to local public opinion and therefore agree to them.

Keeping a factory overmanned for some time may seem wasteful but it has some advantages. First, it helps avoid negative publicity. Second, it allows time to help those who will be laid off - for example, through offering incentives to those who volunteer for early retirement. Wages are generally low in most emerging markets so the overall cost is rarely prohibitive in the scheme of things. But buyers should be aware in advance of closing the deal what the cost will be. You may find scores of workers listed as employees in the books who were registered merely to have time counted towards their pension and to receive social and health benefits. Thorough due diligence should identify the number of such workers.

The third reason for giving short-term employment guarantees is that many firms need time to restructure the acquired business. This allows them to assess individual employees and decide which ones they want to keep and which they would like to be rid of when the guarantee has run its term.

Spinning off certain functions is another way to improve efficiency and eliminate headcount. Acquisition candidates may own their own kindergartens or fire brigades, or are so vertically integrated that the buyer would never want to engage in all of the activities involved. Some spin-offs are small and easy; for example, vehicles can be given to workers from the fire brigade to start their own business. Other spin-offs are more complicated but always possible.

Another way to win over the public and workers is to create good outplacement and retraining programmes for those who are not wanted. The message is clear: "We are not just kicking you out, we will help you acquire new skills and we will try to help you find work elsewhere. Also, once we reach our productivity targets and if production starts to grow, we will need new people and you will be the first ones we will look at." Such an attitude boosts the morale of those who stay because everyone likes to work for an employer who cares.

Ask any M&A consultant why acquisitions often fail and one of the top three responses will always be poor post-acquisition restructuring and integration. Integration is a complex procedure. It involves keeping all acquired employees focused, making sure the best people have good incentives to stay and identifying early any potential personnel conflicts. It also involves merging organisational cultures and structures and engaging new employees in new activities. A skilled integration manager should work closely with an external human resources consultancy specialising in integration issues, of which one of the most critical is to make sure that staff in the acquired company fully understand the objectives of the acquisition, the plan for the future and how it will be implemented.

Acquisitions in emerging countries: some lessons

- ◪ Acquisitions in emerging markets depend on due diligence being conducted thoroughly, so be prepared to invest time, money and human resources in it.
- ◪ Acquisitions in emerging markets make sense if there is a significant market share or brand to buy. They also make sense if they give access to a new market segment or strategically limit the activities of your fiercest competitors (international or domestic).
- ◪ Approach a potential target's managers and get them on your side. In the majority of cases, only managers have real inside knowledge of the enterprise they work in.
- ◪ Looking for the fundamental drivers of future earnings is much more important than number crunching.
- ◪ Use the best characteristics of investigative journalism during the due diligence process. Talk to workers, customers, distributors, suppliers, other companies in the industry, ministries, independent industrial experts and market research agencies.
- ◪ Expect due diligence and negotiations to last a long time and be prepared for setbacks. Persistence and patience pay off.
- ◪ Set up acquisition teams to constantly search for suitable targets.
- ◪ Identify a target's weak points, and make use of them during the negotiation process.
- ◪ Check every number in the financial statements and treat all numbers with caution.

- Have people on the ground from the beginning of the due diligence process. Don't expect things to happen if you are trying to buy "from a distance".
- Focus on real future earnings potential rather than any fixed asset values and adjust earnings potential to the point in time when any direct and indirect government support ends and when market conditions evolve.

Joint ventures

Companies should think not twice but five or six times before deciding to go into a joint-venture deal in any emerging market. The verdict on joint ventures from those who are involved in emerging markets seems to be: only go into them if you have no other choice and/or if you really know how to manage them. Before you do, ask yourself some questions. What can a partner do for us that we cannot do ourselves? Is what the partner offers really not achievable through organic growth or an acquisition? If we enter a joint venture, how easy will it be to turn it into a full-scale acquisition?

Joint ventures are never easy to manage, but there are added complexities in emerging markets. Below is a list of things that companies should pay particular attention to.

- **Financial problems.** Local partners are usually less financially adept than the foreign partner. They may not have enough money to invest if the foreign partner wishes to expand and build more manufacturing capacity, for example. This limits growth opportunity and damages joint ventures.
- **Different strategic objectives.** The strategies and objectives of joint-venture partners are often not aligned. Just as many domestic distributors and importers import anything that will earn them a quick return, many domestic companies will go into partnership with anyone who brings them some technology and offers quick and painless profits.
- **Management clashes.** Different managerial styles and approaches are a frequent cause of problems. Work attitudes and the "way things are done around here" can cause enormous problems.
- **Cultural clashes.** This is a particular problem in emerging markets.
- **Lack of communication.** The two partners fail to communicate

strategies and tactics to achieve joint-venture objectives. Before a deal is signed, it is essential to talk to the local partner about expansion plans and expectations.

- **Transfer pricing disagreements.** In the words of a manager of one firm that set up a joint venture in an emerging market: "We are wondering when they are going to realise that we are ripping them off with our transfer pricing." Well, sooner or later, most local partners learn the tricks and the trouble begins.

11 Dealing with corruption and crime

If the soul is left in darkness, sins will be committed. The guilty one is not he who commits the sin, but he who causes the darkness.

Victor Hugo

It takes a crook to catch a crook.

Franklin Delano Roosevelt, explaining why he hired Joseph K. Kennedy to head the Securities and Exchange Commission

Corruption and crime are constant problems in many emerging markets. In some countries the threats they pose can be serious, even fatal. This chapter outlines the types of corruption and crime that firms may come up against, and explains how to recognise and deal with them. It looks at international efforts to eliminate corruption and explains why so few companies are entirely clean (even if they insist that they are).

Corruption

Dealing with corruption is a daily task in all emerging markets, and the cost for both international companies and developing countries is high. Indeed, the World Bank warns that corruption is the greatest obstacle for economic and social development in developing countries. Numerous studies have shown a strong correlation between a high incidence of crime and corruption and low foreign direct investment. World Bank reports have repeatedly shown that countries with high levels of crime and corruption grow more slowly than cleaner countries, and their share of world trade and exports keeps shrinking.

Government projects may be awarded to incompetent contractors. Money changes hands but the work is never properly done. The country's infrastructure remains poor but its debt balloons. Corrupt regimes often cause economic crises in their countries. In Slovakia in the mid-1990s, for example, the autocratic leader appointed his friends to run state banks and large state companies. Loans were given to enterprises without regard to risk management. Most of the money ended up in companies where directors stripped assets and moved cash offshore to private bank accounts. Local legislation was so immature that technically many of these crony capitalist schemes were not illegal. The subsequent prime minister of Slovakia told an Economist Conferences government roundtable:

> We can't even start prosecuting. The law in those days allowed the scheme. Those that we'd like to prosecute, where we have some evidence of wrongdoing, live abroad in big houses.

Similar crony capitalism is often cited as one of the reasons for the Asian crisis of 1997.

Studies have shown that bribes increase the cost of doing business in emerging markets by 3–10%. If the country has a physical security problem (as in South Africa or some Latin American countries), the cost of doing business can increase by a similar amount. But corruption is not an argument against doing business in emerging markets. First, it is not widespread in emerging markets (see Table 11.1, pages 101–2). Some countries are less corrupt than others, and even in corrupt countries the corruption may be limited to a small number of institutions and individuals. It may also be seasonal, as some individuals try to get rich before their public post expires. It is not difficult to find out about and keep track of who these individuals are and what they demand. Some countries such as Nigeria are rampantly corrupt; others may have less corruption but are harder to deal with because it is not so obvious. Second, it is possible to do business in emerging markets without paying bribes.

Many companies try to stay clean even if this means a loss of business. Some work with third parties and do not care what they do.

American companies complain that European companies pay large commissions to those who secure contracts for them in various emerging markets. European companies say that they had to do it because American political clout could secure lucrative contracts for American companies. Until recently, a number of EU countries allowed companies to treat commissions as a tax deductible expense for international contracts. New OECD (Organisation for Economic Co-operation and Development) legislation has changed this. However, enforcement of this legislation by governments has been patchy.

There is a lot of hypocrisy surrounding the issue. Before the Foreign Corrupt Practices Act (FCPA) came into force in the United States in 1977, the enforcement arm of the Securities and Exchange Commission (SEC) got over 400 American companies to admit to making multimillion-dollar payments to foreign governments directly and indirectly to secure the business. Nowadays, many American companies pride themselves on being super clean and of sticking to the letter of the FCPA, which outlaws bribery of government officials.

However, this does not mean they are not benefiting from corruption. Some companies sell their products to third parties who pay bribes in order to resell them to final buyers or further intermediaries. Thus American products may end up being bought by buyers who would never buy them without a bribe. It is unlikely that these companies do not know what their partners do to sell the products to the final buyers. As one executive says:

> I don't want to know how they do it. I get the money from
> their account in Geneva or the Cayman Islands, we ship the
> goods, and that's where my engagement ends.

Many companies use intermediaries to win tenders, and these intermediaries may pay bribes to secure deals.

This is a breach of the FCPA and the most recent anti-bribery legislation in the UK. Both laws require companies to know what their intermediaries do. Indeed, in a recent groundbreaking bribery case in Lesotho, a German company was charged for allowing a non-employed agent to pay a bribe to an official. By demonstrating that the intermediary's primary purpose was to pay the bribe to win the business and so avoid corporate liability, the judge wiped out the company's defence that it could not be responsible for third parties.

Managers engage in such transactions for a simple reason: they are under pressure to sell more and meet budgets. Cutting corners on the borderline of legality has become normal even for companies that claim publicly to be squeaky clean.

It is important to differentiate between facilitating payments and bribes, although not all legislation makes the distinction. The FCPA does, but the new UK legislation apparently does not. Facilitating payments are made to an individual who demands it for a service that a company would expect to receive without payment in normal commercial circumstances, for example for getting a stamp from a customs official. The FCPA says facilitating payments are made "for routine government action" and accept it as legal. But companies are obliged to report these payments to the authorities, their own company and their embassies.

This is one example of activities on the edge of legality that some observers regard as bribery. But reality is not so black and white. Many companies, including American companies under the scrutiny of the

FCPA, engage in all sorts of activities that are not outright illegal and are intended to get things done in a corrupt environment. Companies sometimes put a corrupt business partner or government official on the books as a consultant. Or they ask them if their sons or daughters would like scholarships for top business schools. Or they invite them to Paris or New York with their families for several weeks of "business negotiations" and give them substantial daily payments. There is a thin line between an envelope full of money and more sophisticated methods.

One regional director offers some practical advice:

> It is possible to do straight business. You have to be ready to lose out on some big sales short-term. But in the end, straight business is better business. If you decide to pay bribes it is like dancing with a gorilla – what do you do when you want to stop?

Most legislative attempts to reduce bribes have largely been in vain. It is hard to police and catch those who do it. In the 25 years since the inception of the FCPA, there have been less than 50 prosecutions. It is particularly hard to monitor remote subsidiaries of large American, EU and Japanese multinationals. Although FCPA and OECD anti-bribery legislation (the latter signed by 35 countries only in 1997 and in force since 1999) sounds encouraging, there seems to be little practical enforcement. According to a 2002 Transparency International survey of more than 800 businesses, the new OECD legislation is failing to make an impact, despite the fact that anyone found breaking the rules can end up in jail. In a rare publicised case, IBM's headquarters found that its subsidiary in Buenos Aires had paid some $4.5m to directors of the state-owned Banco de la Nacion Argentina (via a local subcontractor to whom IBM Argentina paid $22m) to win a contract to install IT systems. The value of the contract was estimated at $250m. Were it not for IBM's own internal controls, the case would never have reached the SEC. However, the fine imposed on IBM was only $300,000; that is, 0.12% of the value of the business it secured with the bribe. The reason for the low fine was the "strong corrective action taken by IBM". The Economist, on March 2nd 2002, wondered if IBM would have had to report the case to the SEC if the bribe had been paid to a privately-owned bank (since such payments are not covered by the FCPA).

Apart from a few companies themselves reporting corruption to the SEC and internally punishing the managers involved, little policing and enforcement actually happens. With the emergence of more accounting scandals, SEC staff seem to have more pressing things to do than pay much attention to bribes being paid thousands of miles away.

UK legislation has been criticised as being full of loopholes, but new anti-bribery legislation became law on January 1st 2004.

Nevertheless, the most effective way to deal with the problem of corruption is through internal corporate controls. Companies should provide clear guidelines for managers who are asked to pay a bribe, including, for example, to whom they should report the incident and what procedures they should follow. Leadership must come from the top. The CEO should implement a zero-tolerance bribery policy and install systems to police and implement it. The message to staff in remote locations should be: "If you are asked to pay a bribe to secure a sale, and not securing it means missing your budget, don't be afraid to tell your partner to look for someone else who will pay the money."

Company leaders need to be aware that if they do not impose tough internal controls, the loss of reputation will affect the company far more than typically low fines for misconduct. Although companies can secure some short-term business through bribery, the loss of reputation will mean long-term damage. They should also be aware that the public increasingly knows what is going on. The World Bank features a list of bribe-payers on its website and does not allow them to bid for any new Bank-related projects.

What is corruption?

If an American congressman gets money from a corporation to lobby for certain corporate interests, this would constitute bribery in many EU countries. An Italian prime minister and a former German chancellor, let alone seven of the last seven Japanese construction ministers, have been investigated for corruption.

The use of offshore tax havens – places where individuals and companies can manage and dispose of capital at minimum cost without political interference and punitive taxes – is denounced when rich Russians are involved. But the media rarely mention the fact that these were created by wealthy industrialised countries for corporate and private tax avoidance. Worse, many offshore havens are not even physically offshore. There are more than 100 of them with offices in New York City alone. Not surprisingly, many companies use the offshore accounts of their partners in emerging markets to do business and get paid quickly.

Crime: individual and organised

A regional manager for Latin America at a large consumer goods company says:

> Some goods were always missing from our truck and
> sometimes the whole truck disappears. Now we employ armed
> security guards to look after the shipments. We had to do it
> since no insurance company would insure the load.

Most security risks are manageable provided that there are clear and detailed security guidelines and precautions, and enough resources to implement them. In risky countries, all new employees should attend a personal security seminar. It is also essential to have a manual detailing security guidelines and procedures on how to prevent and deal with various security threats. This has become one of the most important internal corporate documents in many markets. Companies should develop such manuals systematically. Less experienced firms should learn from those experienced in emerging markets. It is surprising how many companies deal with security in an ad hoc fashion. These companies are clearly vulnerable.

Security guidelines must be detailed. They should cover such matters as what to do if a staff member and his or her family are threatened by local organised crime groups and list the blood group of all employees in case they are wounded. There are many instances in which local employees of multinational companies and their families have been threatened.

There is no doubt that the cost of doing business in many emerging markets is seriously inflated by the need to ensure the physical security of assets and people. Substantial amounts are budgeted each year for security. This is a necessity because investment in security is not only a protective but also a preventive measure. Companies that erect visible security obstacles around their facilities face fewer threats. Gangsters prefer the easy prey.

In a number of countries, it has become usual to drive around in armoured company cars and have bodyguards. If someone is kidnapped, it is wise to listen to the kidnappers' demands. A director of a German company was kidnapped in Russia. A ransom was demanded but not paid. The director was killed. When the German company sent a replacement, he was also kidnapped. A ransom was demanded and this time it was paid. The director was released unharmed.

Companies have come up with many ways of combating criminal

threats. The fight against highway hijacking is turning into a mini industry: as well as employing security guards to follow convoys, goods are increasingly being marked with serial numbers so stolen goods can be tracked more easily. External affairs managers try to work closely with all levels of government and in particular interior ministries. New technologies are used too. A *Financial Times* report from Brazil described trucks equipped with devices that can shut off the fuel supply of stolen vehicles via satellite. But sometimes none of this is enough. Mini armies attack convoys and armed guards prove inadequate. Police officers may turn out to be not just part of the gang but organisers too. However, although the problem remains expensive and frustrating, it is ultimately manageable.

Organised crime is more difficult to deal with than visible security threats. It comes in many guises and is not always easy to recognise. Generally, domestically owned businesses are much easier to attack than multinationals. But organised criminals sometimes target multinationals for extortion and managers should be ready to respond.

One company was approached by what seemed like a well-dressed, legitimate group of local businessmen wanting to talk about co-operation. Gradually, the questioning went beyond matters concerning co-operation and the company grew suspicious. One way of dealing with such threats is to "kill" intruders with corporate bureaucracy. In this example the company brought in legal advisers who asked the intruders polite but legally loaded questions. The manager also kept repeating that on such matters they would have to check with headquarters and that this would take time.

Companies should also be careful when recruiting. Organised crime groups are well known for trying to place people in the target company. The legitimacy of degrees and diplomas should be checked, and security companies may be able to do other pre-hire checks. This is important, especially if the person concerned is likely to have access to certain accounts or banking links.

Table 11.1 **Transparency International rankings**

Rank	Country	CPI 2002 score[a]	Surveys used[b]	Standard deviation[c]	High–low range[d]
1	Finland	9.7	8	0.4	8.9–10.0
2	Denmark	9.5	8	0.3	8.9–9.9
	New Zealand	9.5	8	0.2	8.9–9.6
4	Iceland	9.4	6	0.4	8.8–10.0
5	Singapore	9.3	13	0.2	8.9–9.6
	Sweden	9.3	10	0.2	8.9–9.6
7	Canada	9.0	10	0.2	8.7–9.3
	Luxembourg	9.0	5	0.5	8.5–9.9
	Netherlands	9.0	9	0.3	8.5–9.3
10	United Kingdom	8.7	11	0.5	7.8–9.4
11	Australia	8.6	11	1.0	6.1–9.3
12	Norway	8.5	8	0.9	6.9–9.3
	Switzerland	8.5	9	0.9	6.8–9.4
14	Hong Kong	8.2	11	0.8	6.6–9.4
15	Austria	7.8	8	0.5	7.2–8.7
16	United States	7.7	12	0.8	5.5–8.7
17	Chile	7.5	10	0.9	5.6–8.8
18	Germany	7.3	10	1.0	5.0–8.1
	Israel	7.3	9	0.9	5.2–8.0
20	Belgium	7.1	8	0.9	5.5–8.7
	Japan	7.1	12	0.9	5.5–7.9
	Spain	7.1	10	1.0	5.2–8.9
23	Ireland	6.9	8	0.9	5.5–8.1
24	Botswana	6.4	5	1.5	5.3–8.9
25	France	6.3	10	0.9	4.8–7.8
	Portugal	6.3	9	1.0	5.5–8.0
27	Slovenia	6.0	9	1.4	4.7–8.9
28	Namibia	5.7	5	2.2	3.6–8.9
29	Estonia	5.6	8	0.6	5.2–6.6
	Taiwan	5.6	12	0.8	3.9–6.6
31	Italy	5.2	11	1.1	3.4–7.2
32	Uruguay	5.1	5	0.7	4.2–6.1
33	Hungary	4.9	11	0.5	4.0–5.6
	Malaysia	4.9	11	0.6	3.6–5.7
	Trinidad & Tobago	4.9	4	1.5	3.6–6.9
36	Belarus	4.8	3	1.3	3.3–5.8
	Lithuania	4.8	7	1.9	3.4–7.6
	South Africa	4.8	11	0.5	3.9–5.5
	Tunisia	4.8	5	0.8	3.6–5.6
40	Costa Rica	4.5	6	0.9	3.6–5.9
	Jordan	4.5	5	0.7	3.6–5.2
	Mauritius	4.5	6	0.8	3.5–5.5
	South Korea	4.5	12	1.3	2.1–7.1
44	Greece	4.2	8	0.7	3.7–5.5
45	Brazil	4.0	10	0.4	3.4–4.8
	Bulgaria	4.0	7	0.9	3.3–5.7
	Jamaica	4.0	3	0.4	3.6–4.3
	Peru	4.0	7	0.6	3.2–5.0
	Poland	4.0	11	1.1	2.6–5.5
50	Ghana	3.9	4	1.4	2.7–5.9
51	Croatia	3.8	4	0.2	3.6–4.0
52	Czech Republic	3.7	10	0.8	2.6–5.5
	Latvia	3.7	4	0.2	3.5–3.9
	Morocco	3.7	4	1.8	1.7–5.5
	Slovak Republic	3.7	8	0.6	3.0–4.6

Rank	Country	CPI 2002 score[a]	Surveys used[b]	Standard deviation[c]	High-low range[d]
	Sri Lanka	3.7	4	0.4	3.3–4.3
57	Colombia	3.6	10	0.7	2.6–4.6
	Mexico	3.6	10	0.6	2.5–4.9
59	China	3.5	11	1.0	2.0–5.6
	Dominican Republic	3.5	4	0.4	3.0–3.9
	Ethiopia	3.5	3	0.5	3.0–4.0
62	Egypt	3.4	7	1.3	1.7–5.3
	El Salvador	3.4	6	0.8	2.0–4.2
64	Thailand	3.2	11	0.7	1.5–4.1
	Turkey	3.2	10	0.9	1.9–4.6
66	Senegal	3.1	4	1.7	1.7–5.5
67	Panama	3.0	5	0.8	1.7–3.6
68	Malawi	2.9	4	0.9	2.0–4.0
	Uzbekistan	2.9	4	1.0	2.0–4.1
70	Argentina	2.8	10	0.6	1.7–3.8
71	Côte d'Ivoire	2.7	4	0.8	2.0–3.4
	Honduras	2.7	5	0.6	2.0–3.4
	India	2.7	12	0.4	2.4–3.6
	Russia	2.7	12	1.0	1.5–5.0
	Tanzania	2.7	4	0.7	2.0–3.4
	Zimbabwe	2.7	6	0.5	2.0–3.3
77	Pakistan	2.6	3	1.2	1.7–4.0
	Philippines	2.6	11	0.6	1.7–3.6
	Romania	2.6	7	0.8	1.7–3.6
	Zambia	2.6	4	0.5	2.0–3.2
81	Albania	2.5	3	0.8	1.7–3.3
	Guatemala	2.5	6	0.6	1.7–3.5
	Nicaragua	2.5	5	0.7	1.7–3.4
	Venezuela	2.5	10	0.5	1.5–3.2
85	Georgia	2.4	3	0.7	1.7–2.9
	Ukraine	2.4	6	0.7	1.7–3.8
	Vietnam	2.4	7	0.8	1.5–3.6
88	Kazakhstan	2.3	4	1.1	1.7–3.9
89	Bolivia	2.2	6	0.4	1.7–2.9
	Cameroon	2.2	4	0.7	1.7–3.2
	Ecuador	2.2	7	0.3	1.7–2.6
	Haiti	2.2	3	1.7	0.8–4.0
93	Moldova	2.1	4	0.6	1.7–3.0
	Uganda	2.1	4	0.3	1.9–2.6
95	Azerbaijan	2.0	4	0.3	1.7–2.4
96	Indonesia	1.9	12	0.6	0.8–3.0
	Kenya	1.9	5	0.3	1.7–2.5
98	Angola	1.7	3	0.2	1.6–2.0
	Madagascar	1.7	3	0.7	1.3–2.5
	Paraguay	1.7	3	0.2	1.5–2.0
101	Nigeria	1.6	6	0.6	0.9–2.5
102	Bangladesh	1.2	5	0.7	0.3–2.0

a Corruption Perception Index. Score relates to perceptions of the degree of corruption as seen by business people and risk analysts and ranges between 10 (highly clean) and 0 (highly corrupt).

b The number of surveys that assessed a country's performance. A total of 15 surveys were used from nine independent institutions, and at least three surveys were required for a country to be included in the CPI.

c Indicates differences in the values of the sources: the greater the standard deviation, the greater the differences of perceptions of a country among the sources.

d Provides the highest and lowest values of the different sources.

Source: Transparency International. A more detailed description of the CPI methodology is available at www.transparency.org/cpi/index.html#cpi or at www.gwdg.de/~uwvw/2002.html

12 Human resources: myths and reality

Treat people as if they were what they ought to be and you help them become what they are capable of being.

Johann Wolfgang von Goethe

This chapter explores the issues of attracting, retaining and managing talent in emerging markets. It also analyses the pros and cons of using local staff rather than expatriates.

Experienced companies in emerging markets know that talented and reliable local managers are essential for success, and they try to remove expatriate managers as soon as possible. But finding and keeping such people in emerging markets is hard for one overwhelming reason: the pool of local talent is shallow. With typically strong demand and weak supply, it is no wonder that multinationals are forced to pay top salaries to local managers. Despite overall low labour costs in emerging markets, it is not uncommon for, say, a finance manager in Poland or Hungary to earn more than his peers in Germany or the UK.

Many companies are unwilling to adjust their global corporate pay scales to the local circumstances of supply and demand. But if a company refuses to pay the Hungarian finance manager more than its British one, it will have to settle for a person of average ability running its finances in Hungary. Another option is to fill the difficult positions with an expatriate, but this is generally even more expensive, considering all the benefits that are included in a typical expatriate package. Furthermore, it is only a local who will know the market best and will be able to establish something that expatriates often mismanage: personal relationships with customers, partners and government ministers and officials.

Expatriates, if needed, should be carefully selected. A successful manager in the United States does not necessarily translate into a successful manager in Turkey or India. During the selection process it is necessary to look for two important ingredients: international exposure and a passion for new environments and cultures. It is no use transferring an excellent American manager who has never travelled abroad and is not pushing for an international expatriate assignment.

Companies with large operations in certain emerging-market regions have started relocating experienced managers from one country to build up business in a less-developed market in the same region. The knowledge transfer often works better than with managers from developed markets, but companies need to be aware of cultural sensitivities. It may, for example, be acceptable to give an American manager a generous expatriate package, but giving the same package to a manager from a neighbouring country may cause problems. A solution is to introduce regional expatriate packages that cover relocation costs but offer fewer frills.

Once on the ground, expatriates are usually replaced too often. As soon as they settle down, develop some local relationships, start (maybe) speaking the local language and gain trust from local business partners and employees, they are sent to a new location. The process of integrating a new expatriate then starts all over again. Such rapid turnover of expatriate staff and lack of continuity are bad for business.

Many successful companies start with expatriates but set up a system of searching for a local replacement early on. Top local talent is trained to take over, with intensive mentoring and coaching. It is a paradox these days that expatriate country managers must train locals so they can eliminate their own position. In these difficult economic times many expatriates simply try to slow down the process of replacement. They fear (in many cases rightly) that once there is a capable replacement *in situ*, there will be nowhere for them to return or go to. Even if they do return to the home country, seasoned expatriates know that it will not be easy. Many say that working again in the developed world is boring and predictable. Some are unable to readjust to the old way of living. Most, of course, miss the generous expatriate packages and luxurious standard of living. It is not unusual to hear expatriate managers reporting to the top: "This local guy I've been training to take over is really great but I don't think he is ready yet. Here are the reasons why ... I think I need to stay here a little longer." Needless to say, in the more dangerous locations in emerging markets, expatriates on assignment often cannot wait to get out.

Once an emerging market starts developing, the supply of skilled labour improves. New universities offer new programmes, which are better tailored to the real world and the needs of companies. With time, an increase in supply inevitably reduces the relative price of skilled managers. But in many markets, a shortage of skilled local labour continues for a long time.

Finding local managers

There is no magic formula for finding local managers, but the following methods may help.

Establish good links to universities

Many companies prefer to hire new graduates, who can be trained to be good corporate soldiers. To identify the best students and get to them early, companies set up links with universities, funding certain programmes and offering internships to students who have not yet graduated. Many successful companies fund scholarships for the most talented students.

Use locally based headhunters

Many successful companies rely on headhunters to find the best. Locally based human resources consultants (not necessarily local companies) usually offer a better service than those trying to operate from a distance. Their local contacts are better and they are better able to assess candidates' skills for a specific local market.

Invest in corporate brand building

Like western products and brands, company names often mean little in emerging markets. It is important to do some brand building for the company as a whole so that talented jobseekers understand who you are and why they should want to work for you. The process of building a company name in a local market should not be underestimated. A manager at Diageo, the company formed by the merger of Guinness and Grand Metropolitan, tells the story of his empty stand at a Budapest jobs fair. Perplexed by the lack of interest, he collared a student and asked him what the problem was. "Why should I want to work for a Hungarian carpet firm?" the student asked. The manager realised that nobody knew what Diageo was. He went to a bar and brought back Guinness, Bailey's and Smirnoff and was soon surrounded by hundreds of potential applicants. (Whether this was a result of brand recognition or thirst is beside the point.) Because skilled talent is scarce, the best people are keen to work for companies with a good name and reputation. If your company name is not known locally, you will find it difficult to attract the best. Companies preparing for market entry and market expansion should see the cost of making potential employees aware of your brand and your products as a necessary investment and plan for it.

Hire from other multinationals

The downside for companies that train young graduates is that they often lose them to "poachers" from other companies. Extensive job hopping and poaching are the norm in many emerging markets.

Participate in job fairs

Job fairs and careers days present the company to young local people seeking work, and it is worth taking part in them. However, it is hard to stand out from the crowd, and the method is more reactive than proactive. There is a strong chance that the best candidates will have been pre-selected by proactive companies, leaving you with more average ones.

Retention strategies

Because the pool of skilled workers is shallower than in developed countries, retention strategies require a different approach. In many emerging markets, staff retention is a bigger challenge than staff selection. Some successful multinationals admit that local managers they are keen to keep in developing countries often enjoy far superior packages to managers at the same level in developed countries. As well as a salary that exceeds the local average for the post, for example, standard benefits will include performance-related bonuses, private health insurance and private pensions. These are often topped up with loans to buy or renovate homes (either direct company loans or through an outside institution, with the company often subsidising interest rates); share ownership (even if an employee at that level in the developed country would never receive any shares); company cars (again at a junior level); and membership of gyms and sports clubs. Employees take it for granted that the company will provide a clear career path, continuous training opportunities, mentoring and coaching, as well as allowing for a balance between work and private life.

It is important that senior managers know what local salaries and packages for skilled managers are before market entry. Clearly, there are markets where compensation for local managers will be a substantial cost, higher than in a developed country. Senior managers must be flexible and allow adjustments (if necessary) of global pay and benefits scales. Imposing a global scale on a heated emerging market is a great way to lose great staff.

Most companies acknowledge that it is dangerous to underpay relative to market averages, but most are wary of paying much more than the average. They feel it is dangerous to enter a pay race because there will always be a company that will offer something more (a bigger starting salary, a bigger bonus or a more generous private pension). Multinationals increasingly find that competition for skilled people comes from unexpected sources. In Russia, for example, large domestic firms in the hands of new "robber barons" now pay young MBA graduates twice as much as large multinational companies do. Many companies, unwilling or unable to pay such premium rates, now focus their retention strategies on other aspects of job satisfaction. There is a widely held view that it makes sense to conduct employee and/or job satisfaction surveys more often in emerging markets than in developed countries. With continued shortages of skilled workers, the wants and needs of those with the required skills change frequently, so it is useful to keep track of signs of job dissatisfaction.

Tracking salaries

Keeping track of salary movements is tricky. Levels change quickly, rocketing upwards in good times and sliding rapidly downwards in times of crisis. Wage levels often have nothing to do with broad economic indicators, such as inflation or GDP per head. For example, white-collar salaries in Slovakia tripled between 1995 and 2002. At the same time, prices in the economy in general went up about 50%.

In countries with a history of economic crisis or those that are potentially vulnerable to devaluation, it is wise to avoid paying salaries linked to dollars or euros. When crisis strikes, the hard-currency link boosts fixed costs at a time of declining revenues (when converted into hard-currency earnings).

Important aspects of job satisfaction other than pay in emerging markets include the following.

- Career planning with a clear path, ideally in combination with international assignments and later permanent international responsibility.
- Training and development covering all aspects of business,

including soft-skills training (such as communications, cultural training, leadership skills and stress management).

◪ Performance management, including coaching, mentoring, regular feedback, good communications and appraisals.

◪ Providing a good balance between work and leisure time

13 Corporate social responsibility

With great powers come great responsibilities ... The inhibitions placed on the irresponsible use of technology are weak, often half-hearted, and almost always, worldwide, subordinated to short-term national or corporate interest.

Carl Sagan

Many companies have run into trouble as a result of criticism of their standards of what in the jargon is termed corporate social responsibility; for example, over working conditions in their factories or the use of child labour. This chapter gives practical advice on what companies should be aware of and what action they should take to help improve the bottom line and avoid damaging bad publicity.

"The sea is alive," said a print advertisement signed (in small print) by Coca-Cola Beverages (one of Coca-Cola's largest bottlers). The text of the advertisement told the story of a group of kindergarten children taught by two young marine biologists, learning about animals living in the sea and learning that the sea has to be kept clean to keep these animals alive. It went on to say that the company supports ecological education and any action that protects the environment. There were photos of children sitting on the beach listening to the two young scientists in their wet suits. None of the children were drinking Coke. The Coke logo was in fairly small print.

This is just one creative example where corporate social responsibility (CSR) and brand building become one. Those who see the advertisement get a "feel-good" sensation about the company and the brand. It is also a clever, subtle way to sell the product.

But how many companies really use CSR to help their business? Imagine you need to fill your tank and there is a choice between several fuel stations along the road. Would you avoid, say, Shell because the company was accused by pressure groups of wanting to sink one of its old oil platforms in the sea? Would you really care if the price of fuel was cheaper at Shell than at other filling stations?

This is the kind of dilemma that many companies face. If they invest a lot of money in CSR, will it really affect their business? If they invest nothing in CSR, will it make any difference?

In emerging markets, many citizens are cynical about and sometimes hostile to "the big fat capitalists coming to exploit us". Many companies witness high levels of scepticism and hostility during and after market entry. Well thought through and active CSR with substance can prevent this.

In a 2003 survey of CEOs conducted by the consultancy arm of PricewaterhouseCoopers, one of the big four accountancy firms, 79% of respondents believed that CSR was crucial for profitability. This is an increase of some 10% compared with the previous year. Awareness of CSR at the top of the corporate hierarchy seems to be increasing. However, critics say that CEOs are just paying lip-service to CSR and that there is little substance in their actions. The reason is simple – there is no clear link between short-term profitability (an overwhelming concern to most CEOs) and spending on CSR.

Despite some improvements, many international companies still neglect CSR. Some have already suffered bad publicity, which has affected their sales, profits and share price. Companies that have ignored the environment or working conditions or working practices in their emerging-market operations (generally where manufacturing has been outsourced to local third parties) have suffered the most. For example, some multinationals were censured in the media when it was alleged that they were using child labour. International companies are now under the tough scrutiny of a plethora of organisations, pressure groups and anti-globalisation protesters.

Companies should have a clear strategy and tools for implementing CSR, especially in emerging markets. It can and should be used as a business tool to build brands, gain a good reputation and minimise the risk of bad publicity. Over time, such actions do have an impact on revenues and profits. If a company systematically builds a public image as a good corporate citizen, it will be in a better position to weather any storm of bad publicity. Furthermore, although surveys have shown that only 20% of consumers will punish companies that are not good corporate citizens by not buying their products, they also show that almost 80% of consumers are more likely to buy products manufactured by good corporate citizens.

But to be effective a CSR strategy must be supported at all corporate levels, most importantly the top. Many companies take a half-hearted approach to CSR, giving it a low priority or treating it as "window dressing". It is companies in so-called controversial industries, such as tobacco, oil or alcohol, which have as a group made the biggest advances in terms of internal "buy in" and getting all to recognise the strategic necessity of having an active CSR approach.

How to create a genuine CSR strategy

There has to be a clear commitment at the top, but not just a statement from the CEO. "Buy in" has to be genuine at all levels, and all business leaders should be involved in the creation of a meaningful strategy that will have an impact on the top and bottom lines. "I don't have time for this nonsense! I have a business to run," said a country manager of a large multinational when asked about CSR in his company. No wonder, perhaps. The economic environment is tough, and the pressures of keeping the business running are too high for managers to focus on what they see as the intangible and uncertain benefits of CSR. This is why many companies wanting to get a genuine CSR strategy off the ground have used the services of consultants specialising in change management.

Best practice is to have a dedicated global CSR co-ordinator working with marketing and PR teams or, in some cases, local people with responsibility for CSR (some tobacco companies have them). As consumers become more socially aware, they are increasingly linking a company's name and its brands to CSR. If a company has a bad image, this will rub off on its brands.

The pressure on companies to be good corporate citizens has spread to more and more areas. The *Financial Times* ("Bitter taste of success", March 11th 2002) reported that Starbucks was being pursued by the US Organic Consumer Association for paying low wages to coffee farmers in emerging countries. The association demanded third-party verified proof that the company does donate money to clinics, schools and credit schemes in coffee-growing communities and that it pays them more than the regular coffee market price. It also told Starbucks not to use milk with Recombinant Bovine Somatotropin (rbST), a growth hormone (although it is approved by the Food and Drugs Administration).

How should companies respond in such circumstances? Starbucks got it right by being diplomatic and not arrogant when responding to these accusations. The last thing a company should do is to make enemies in the community of pressure groups and protesters. Ideally, every effort should be made to listen to their concerns, to communicate and to come up with good arguments to explain why certain demands may be unreasonable. However, where demands make sense, companies can create joint initiatives with pressure groups, and by working as partners bolster the brand.

The benefits for companies that behave as good corporate citizens are clear. After the stockmarket bubble burst, many investors said they were only interested in buying long-term sustainable businesses with an effective CSR policy. There are already funds which invest in companies with good CSR credentials, and they have a growing following and are growing in number. There are also internal corporate benefits. Studies have shown that companies with strong CSR have lower staff turnover and this helps the bottom line.

Some companies still regard CSR as a costly exercise with no proof of tangible benefits. Yet those who do spend on CSR admit (off the record) that the amount they spend is a tiny fraction of their local profit in certain countries. Although it may be difficult to show that CSR boosts profits, particularly in the short term, it does – if it is genuine and well thought out – act as an insurance policy, providing protection against serious business risk. Managers may not like the CSR responsibilities, but it is important that they work closely with certain non-governmental pressure groups, whose influence should not be underestimated.

Other companies are suggesting a radical rethink of branding strategies around CSR issues. Global Legacy, an organisation run by Craig Cohon, a former Coca-Cola marketing executive, proposes that companies should view CSR as an active part of their marketing strategy. "Why not link brand to eradication of urban poverty or fighting against AIDS, for example?" Cohon asks. The same argument could be used for many other areas in emerging markets where the need for improvement is recognised, such as health, education, nutrition and water sanitation.

What a CSR strategy should contain

There are many things that companies do in emerging markets to show they care. These include:

- donating money and equipment to hospitals, universities, schools, kindergartens and orphanages;
- donating money and equipment for environmental clean-up programmes;
- financing vaccination programmes;
- creating scholarships for students;
- donating buses or ambulances to cities or trucks to local fire brigades;
- donating food and vitamin drinks to schoolchildren in poor countries;
- supporting local sporting events which might cease without corporate donations.

But companies need to think of new ways to link CSR activity with brand and corporate image. Bring in all employees to brainstorm. What is it that would really make a difference to the local community? What is urgent and badly needed? Do this frequently, not just once a year.

It is also crucial to make sure the public knows that you are good corporate citizens. Every time you do something, splash it all over the media. This can go further.

- Make the media aware of the financial contribution you are making to the country.
- Get journalists to talk to your blue-collar workers so they see you treat them well and pay fairly and on time.
- Tell local and international journalists how many jobs were created directly and indirectly because of your presence in the country. In case you need to lay off workers, create an outplacement and/or retraining centre to help them find new jobs.

One major area of pressure on companies in emerging markets is poor working conditions and child labour. Conditions must be acceptable, and this often means better than those laid down by law. This includes the conditions in operations run by subcontractors, which can be more difficult to control. Facilities should be inspected regularly. It is not enough for company representatives to visit a factory, check if quality and quantity are acceptable and leave. It is essential to talk to workers, hear their concerns and take action to improve things where necessary. Some companies have hired outside investigators to check how subcontractors treat workers and then acted on the findings.

This is how workers described working conditions to an investigative journalist in one of the Indonesian factories (apparently Taiwanese owned) working for a large American clothing company:

If you want to go to the toilet you have to be lucky. If the supervisor says no, you wet your pants.

In another subcontractor's manufacturing facility, the women regularly worked 18-hour shifts without a break, journalists discovered. When a supply deadline approached, they were given amphetamines to drink, and they were fined for yawning in case someone saw them. Company inspectors were often in the plant, but the subcontractor fined workers for telling the truth.

This is the problem. Most companies have a code of conduct, which, on paper, protects workers' basic rights. But what happens in practice is too often very different, particularly in poor countries and in labour-intensive manufacturing. To prevent bad publicity, many newly socially aware companies now have full-time staff monitoring working conditions where manufacturing is outsourced.

Many economists argue that working in these conditions is better than having no job. "If workers are so unhappy, why do they work there?" they say. "Without foreign manufacturers, they would probably dig through the bins and starve. Now at least they can afford a less miserable way of life." There were sweatshops during the industrial revolution in western Europe and the United States, many argue, so why should it be different this time? Early in the 20th century, they say, it was still common to find child labourers in factories and on farms in many European countries, so why shouldn't a child work in Indonesia if this pays for the food for survival?

Whatever the merits of these arguments, companies should be cautious about the business implications of bad publicity. Not paying enough attention to workers' conditions could come to haunt them as public scrutiny intensifies. No one wants their brand identified with cruel working conditions.

14 Understanding and coping with emerging-market crises

The single most important thing that prevents us from meeting our targets in emerging markets is unpredictable devaluations.

Regional director, Procter & Gamble

Some of my markets are submerging, not emerging.

Regional vice-president, Bacardi-Martini

Think hard before you retrench in a crisis. If you stay you will have more loyal staff, be able to hire the best others lay off, and you will win new customers.

Regional director, Du Pont

In the 1990s crises hit Mexico (1994), Thailand and other Asian countries (1997), Russia (1998) and Brazil (1999). In the early 2000s it was Argentina's turn. Volatility is a characteristic of emerging markets. This chapter looks at the main causes and effects of such crises and considers the likelihood of them becoming less frequent and more predictable. Conventional wisdom suggests that companies should retrench during severe crises, and so retrenchment options are outlined. So too are the alternatives, with reference to companies that have reaped huge benefits by choosing to stay put or expand in times of economic crisis.

Crises in emerging markets are more frequent and more severe than in the developed world. But why do they happen? More worryingly, why do they spread so quickly, even to supposedly well-managed countries? What is the likelihood of a new crisis somewhere and where will it hit next? Managers living and operating in many emerging markets worry about these questions all the time.

Countries hit by a crisis suffer disproportionately, but the majority bounce back, many of them much faster than anyone would have expected.

Mexico

The Mexican collapse was serious. Economists who track recessions say this was one of the worst crises since the Great Depression in the United

States. Worse, the crisis spread to the rest of a traditionally volatile Latin America. What happened?

Foreign investors fell in love with Mexico in the late 1980s and early 1990s. The country's debt crisis was resolved. Mexico, the United States and Canada started to negotiate a North American Free Trade Agreement (NAFTA). The Mexican government was run by economists who were trained at leading American universities. Optimism and enthusiasm spread in the multinational business community as policies grew more liberal and macroeconomic stability seemed impossible to shatter.

But the seeds of instability were already being sown. The inflation rate stayed relatively high and, with a stable exchange rate, there was continuous real appreciation of the currency. As a result, Mexican exports gradually became less competitive. At the same time, as long-standing import barriers were dismantled and more multinationals started to push sales more aggressively (to buyers who felt richer because their currency had in effect become stronger), an import boom was inevitable. To add fuel to the fire, banks started to loan more and more money, which further encouraged demand for imports.

Economists started to worry that the situation was unsustainable and argued for a devaluation to restore competitiveness and push GDP growth higher than population growth. With foreign reserves decreasing, Mexico decided to devalue. But as Paul Krugman, a professor of economics at Princeton University, argued in his book *The Return of Depression Economics*, the authorities made several mistakes and failed to follow the golden rules. First, if a country decides to devalue, the devaluation has to be big enough to prevent speculators from betting on a further decline. Mexico devalued much less than economists and (nervous) markets expected. Second, after the devaluation, the authorities must appear fully in control of economic policies, or nervous investors might start to panic. As well as not following the golden rules, it emerged that certain Mexican businessmen were given inside information about the devaluation and that they profited from it. Soon foreign investors panicked, prompting a large flight of capital out of the country.

Once foreign portfolio capital starts stampeding out of a country (as later happened in Asia and elsewhere), it is hard to stop it. Panic sales of securities denominated in a local currency are quick, often irrational and ruthless, leaving the currency exposed to sharp falls. Investors all want out at the same time, as they try to minimise losses from a falling currency. The Mexican peso quickly lost half of its value. To convince investors to stay in the peso, interest rates reached almost 80%. Another problem fuelled the panic: Mexico had a large dollarised short-term debt and, with the peso weak, the debt ballooned.

Looking back, it is clear that a powerful force was at work, one frequently underestimated by economists obsessed with numbers rather than human behaviour: market psychology or market sentiment. "People value the comfort of the herd," wrote *The Economist*. Psychology would come to play an even bigger role in subsequent emerging-market crises, but in 1994 it received little attention in economic circles. Tellingly, in 2002 the Nobel prize for economics went to Daniel Kahneman, a psychologist, and Vernon Smith, an economist, for their work on market psychology.

Market sentiment on Mexico changed from enthusiasm to panic virtually overnight. When that happens, exchange rate overshooting is inevitable (as masterfully explained in an economics paper written by the late Rudiger Dornbusch, when he was professor of economics at MIT) and rationality goes out of the window.

It is not just financial markets that are hit; the whole economy is too. In Mexico sales – particularly those of multinationals – slumped together with the peso. The foreign banks that in the heady days had lent large sums to local banks and enterprises panicked too. They demanded immediate repayment and shut down new credit lines, exacerbating economic decline and accelerating the fall of the peso, which Mexican banks were forced to sell in order to repay their dollar loans. Many found they did not have enough cash so they made their local borrowers repay their loans.

The pattern has been repeated frequently since. In some cases, as in Argentina and Uruguay in 2002, consumers also panic and withdraw deposits. Whenever there is a run on a bank, the crisis becomes more entrenched and more difficult to recover from. Mexico avoided complete collapse thanks to financial support from the United States and the IMF. Companies operating in Mexico had a tough two years before the corner to recovery was turned. Had the United States not intervened, Mexico would probably have faced a repeat of its 1980s crisis, which lasted some eight years.

Managers running multinationals drew three worrying conclusions as the Mexican crisis unravelled and spread to the rest of Latin America. First, if it could happen in Mexico, which had a sound government and lacked fundamental economic problems, it could probably happen in any emerging country. Second, even an apparently firmly rooted positive perception of a market among media and analysts can change remarkably rapidly. Third, the policy mistakes that set off the crisis had a disproportionately negative effect, but the bounce-back came sooner than anyone anticipated.

These are the lessons of Mexico, but the Asian crisis in 1997 was even more complicated. Market sentiment was still to show its darker side.

Asia

The Asian crisis of 1997 was immense and unexpected. The way it spread from the small Thai economy to the rest of the region was frightening. Overnight, multinational companies went into crisis-management mode.

Pinpointing the reasons for the crisis is not easy. A number of South-East Asian economies had been growing rapidly for over two decades. Growth rates were so high that GDP doubled every decade in some countries. Most economists were entranced. But some economists questioned the growth figures and argued that the growth was based on bringing more people into the workforce and investing in physical capital and infrastructure. They found little evidence that productivity (output per unit of input) was going up in parallel. As economic theory argues, if growth is based only on growth in inputs, it is unsustainable, and the fast growth rates of the past, they concluded, are unlikely to be repeated.

Inputs alone are not enough

Low productivity gain is one of the main reasons the former communist bloc stayed so poor for so long. Productivity gains were small because technological advances were slow and were confined to the military or university science departments. The root cause was that the system did not provide any incentive to innovate or to work.

Although this research offered a view on a future period of lower growth in Asia, there was no reason to suspect that this slowdown would cause a full-blown regional crisis. What happened? One explanation is crony capitalism, which exists in many other emerging markets. Crony capitalism is simple in its perversity and has many facets. For example, a group of friends or the family of the autocratic leader of a developing country gain control over state-owned banks which channel "loans" to other friends who, thanks to the loans, gain control over large enterprises. Assets get stripped and billions end up in private off-shore bank accounts. Some of the money trickles back in a process called "the return of flight capital", but most of the capital does not return. "Loans" are not repaid; banks fail and are often bailed out by unsuspecting taxpayers. But cronyism is not a recent phenomenon and so it cannot explain why the crisis happened at that particular time and why it was so severe and so contagious.

Like Mexico, Thailand went from boom to bust in a very short period, through a typical currency crisis. Thailand shared in the emerging-markets enthusiasm of the early 1990s. The Latin American debt crisis was over, Mexico was a miracle, Asia was full of tiger economies and central and eastern Europe offered an unprecedented opening into a vast territory. Capital flowed happily to Thailand, mostly in bank loans and portfolio investment. But such portfolio capital can easily flee the country if market sentiment changes. As capital was flowing in, demand for the baht soared. The central bank, fearing that exports would suffer if the baht appreciated much in value, tried to preserve a fixed exchange rate. To meet the demand for more baht, it had to print more and sell it in exchange for foreign currency. No central bank likes a credit boom, but in this case it was particularly worrying. Domestic loans poured into the real-estate market, which was overheating. The central bank tried to reduce the money supply by selling government securities to mop up excess baht liquidity. But the scheme backfired. The new government securities were attractive to foreign buyers, returns increased and demand grew. The credit, imports and wage boom continued. The current-account deficit catapulted to levels that made markets nervous. It was then that crony capitalism kicked in, as corrupt banks lent recklessly to corrupt companies without caring about the risk. Foreign bankers made matters worse by continuing to lend to local banks, believing – correctly – that the government (with the help of multilaterals) would bail out such politically well-connected banks.

Observers became nervous. It was clear that if the boom continued it would inevitably drag the country into a currency crisis. When the first crony investments started to lose money, foreign lenders and institutional investors stopped pumping money into Thailand. The real-estate bubble burst and, as in Mexico, the boom turned to bust. Demand for the baht collapsed, and the central bank suddenly faced a different kind of problem. If it let the currency fall, it would worsen the indebtedness of local players because many owed foreign currency to their foreign lenders. A depreciation would also have serious implications for the real economy. However, if the central bank intervened to support the baht by selling its accumulated foreign-exchange reserves, it feared that the resulting reduction of the domestic money supply would make the recession worse (interest rates would certainly go up as a result).

Once a country faces a dilemma like this it becomes easy prey for currency speculators. Why not borrow baht, convert them promptly into dollars at a stable rate, sit on dollars, still owe baht, order a drink, sit on the beach, call a journalist friend to write a story that the baht is about to fall, wait for the baht to collapse, return the baht loan and walk away with a fortune.

At the same time, domestic businesses start to worry about a depreciation, so they carry out the same exercise as the speculators in order to pay back any dollar-denominated debt. In short, no one wanted to hold baht any more. When everyone could see that government intervention to support the baht was quickly exhausting the foreign-exchange reserves, the baht fell much more than expected and the government had to raise interest rates to persuade people to keep baht. So those with loans in dollars and in baht were affected: the former because the weaker baht made the dollar loans more expensive; and the latter because the interest rates on baht loans increased. With high interest rates and a weak currency, the recession hit the real economy and any multinational companies selling in the domestic market.

The Thai crisis started to spread to other Asian countries. Economic theories of contagion had always posited trade links as the main conduit. But the crisis spread to countries with which Thailand had few if any trading links. The main route for contagion was via western financial markets. Although it might be argued that a crisis in Thailand is no reason to pull money out of other Asian markets, many big banks and institutional investors in the West treated Asia as one emerging market (as they did with Latin America). They made little meaningful distinction between national markets and acted on a regional basis (which they are less prone to do these days). They also needed to compensate for losses in Thailand. Curiously, as the crisis spread within Asia, currencies in some central European economies also fell by 10–15%. The reason was similar: investors were looking at profitable markets and pulled out to cover for losses in Asia. Many simply said: "Forget about emerging markets. Just reduce exposure in all of them."

Would capital controls help avoid crises?

Why do all emerging-market countries allow hot capital (short-term portfolio investment, for example) to enter and exit so freely? West European countries did not fully liberalise controls on capital-account movements (particularly short-term ones) for decades after the second world war. Most of them liberalised gradually after reaching a certain level of wealth and stability, and mostly only well into the 1980s and 1990s. In 1993 Maria Schaumayer, a former central bank governor of Austria, said: "The last thing we wanted to liberalise was international capital-account movements." Austria fully liberalised capital-account movements only in November 1991, when it was already one of the wealthiest and most stable countries in the world. It liberalised its capital account fully only when its GDP per head reached some $24,000. In other words, many west European economies were able to develop without facing the risk that speculative capital inflows and outflows carry.

Would the crises in Mexico and Asia have been so severe without such large and volatile foreign capital inflows and outflows? Many economists argue that there would not have been a crisis were it not for panic hot capital outflows. Countries – such as China, India, Chile and Slovenia – that had capital controls in place during emerging-market crises which might have spread to them stayed clear of contagion. So there seems to be some evidence that limited capital controls on speculative movements may act as a buffer against economic crises. According to Frank Rogoff, a former chief economist of the IMF:

> The IMF may have sometimes tilted too far towards benign neglect as countries prematurely liberalised markets for short-term capital movements, before the internal regulatory structure was in place to handle them.

But at the same time, he argues, it is becoming more difficult to enforce capital controls (even if they exist), and to some degree, capital-account and trade liberalisation go hand in hand.

Among economists who question this view, the most prominent is Joseph Stiglitz, a Nobel prize winner, whose book *Globalisation and its Discontents*, published in 2001, summed up his disillusionment with the IMF/World Bank consensus. He argues that "excessively rapid financial and capital market liberalisation was probably the single most important cause of the [Asian] crisis". Did the fact that Austria had capital-account controls until 1991 hinder its record on trade, foreign direct investment (FDI), economic growth and wealth accumulation? Not really. So the question is why a developing country (which is far from being wealthy and stable) should allow any foreigner to buy or borrow its currency for a purpose that is not beneficial for the real local economy. In other words, why not have free capital movements in the case of productive FDI but only gradual lifting of controls on "unproductive" portfolio investment? These questions will continue to be debated for many years.

Financial market players claim that offshore schemes can easily disguise speculative capital as FDI and that local authorities would not be able to tell the difference. There are indeed many tricks, but when Malaysia controversially introduced limited capital controls in September 1998, they proved mostly effective even against such speculative transactions. Others claim that controls are a great way for a few local politicians to enrich themselves. This is true, but corruption exists anyway and using capital controls is just one of many ways for the powerful elite to get rich. Elimination of capital controls does not eliminate corruption. It is worth remembering, however, that if emerging-market economies systematically reduced their financing requirements, they would be less exposed to these hot money flows.

Much of the debate on recent crises has focused on how the IMF responded to them and if its prescribed medicine made them worse. The debate is a heated one, and it is interesting to reflect on how developed markets react to economic downturns. American companies would have been furious if the Federal Reserve had not reduced interest rates following the bursting of the stockmarket bubble and subsequent economic slowdown. Those who live in the developed world take it for granted that central banks reduce interest rates in the face of a downturn. They also expect governments to spend a bit more to support recovery (short-term increase in fiscal spending) and to cut taxes.

But what did the IMF recommend when Asian economies were threatened by a crisis? It suggested raising interest rates and cutting fiscal spending (and even closing some banks). Credit-rating agencies (which have an influence on market perceptions) often take the same line. Fitch, for example, in its report on Mexico in late 2001, said that the country should consider cutting spending because it seemed its economy was slowing down. Would Fitch give the same advice to the United States? Ironically, Mexico's economy was responding to a sharp slowdown in the United States, its key trading partner.

Why does the IMF give advice like this, and what have been the consequences of such advice for the economies that implemented it? The IMF claims that when a crisis strikes, it is like a paramedic in a battlefield, trying to stop the bleeding. At such times, when capital wants to take flight, the primary aim is to restore confidence in the market to enable economic stability to return. So to preserve or restore confidence, the IMF orders remedies that go against the kind of Keynesian policies that are widely practised in the developed world. There is a lingering question in all this. Would there be a need to preserve market confidence (by raising interest rates sharply and cutting fiscal spending) if some capital controls on certain hot money movements existed?

A paper entitled "Did Malaysian Capital Controls Work?", written by Ethan Kaplan and Dani Rodrik of Harvard University, appeared in 2001. It analysed what happened during the 1997 Asian crisis to South Korea and Thailand, which implemented the IMF's advice, compared with Malaysia, which introduced short-term capital controls on portfolio capital (not FDI or profit repatriation, for example). Importantly, the comparison was made at the moment the IMF's policies were implemented in other countries and Malaysia (which was continually slipping into crisis) introduced its capital controls. In their conclusions Kaplan and Rodrik state:

> Compared to IMF programmes, we find that the Malaysian policies produced faster economic recovery, smaller declines in employment and real wages, and more rapid turnaround in the stockmarket.

Incidentally, as well as implementing limited short-term capital controls, Malaysia reversed its initial response to the crisis which included raising interest rates and cutting spending.

South Korea and Thailand (both of which followed IMF advice) saw their economies begin to recover once confidence was restored, but their recovery took longer. Many argue that the severe slump they suffered might have been avoided if limited capital controls had been in place, preventing a sudden flight of short-term capital. China, despite high levels of corruption and an imperfect banking system, avoided the Asian crisis. You could not buy the local currency unless you had a good reason to do so.

The debate on capital controls is lively, but a consensus is emerging that certain capital controls were lifted too soon. Jeffrey Sachs of

Harvard University argues that interest rates should not have been raised and that this would have resulted in only modest devaluations. Furthermore, not introducing draconian measures overnight would have caused less panic and that in itself would have stopped the currency slide at a better level.

Something similar happened in Brazil in 1999 proving Sachs's point (which is standard in the developed world). As markets started to lose their "confidence", the authorities devalued by 8%. This was not enough to reassure nervous investors and eventually the central bank stopped intervening. The currency stabilised spontaneously at a somewhat lower level and the stockmarket jumped by a third. Suddenly, investors started to believe in Brazil and the prospect of lower interest rates, which would drive recovery. Two days later, the IMF insisted to surprised Brazilian officials that to achieve real restoration of market confidence, interest rates should be raised further. The next day the Brazilian government announced that it would not lower interest rates and the currency plunged. In *The Return of Depression Economics*, Krugman says:

> *What seems to have happened is that Washington officials*
> *had become so committed to the idea that one must always*
> *raise interest rates to defend the currency that they could not*
> *bring themselves to consider the alternative.*

But even small devaluations in some countries can create enormous problems. For example, in many countries a fall in the currency feeds the inflation rate as people (who are used to currency instability) "think" in hard currency. Also, in cases when there are large foreign currency debts, a devaluation increases the debt and creates all sorts of economic problems.

The IMF usually advises countries to undertake certain structural reforms as a precondition for financial help. It is impossible to find a country in the world that does not have some sort of structural problem – for example, look at the Japanese banking system or EU labour laws. But a growing number of economists argue that although it is important to solve structural problems, this can be done more easily in an environment that does not create sharp recessions as a result of high interest rates, severe cuts in spending, higher taxes and orders to shut down certain banks. Moreover, insisting on structural reforms as part of a short-term package creates unrealistic deadlines, making market players even more nervous.

So why were capital flows liberalised so soon in so many developing countries? Some blame the influence of Wall Street bankers, who saw an opportunity to make money. Some even claim it is part of a western conspiracy to economically control (recolonise) the developing world.

Whatever the explanation, many are irritated by the IMF's double standards. Turkey, which rarely fulfils any promises it makes to the IMF, was regularly receiving substantial amounts of bail-out money. Meanwhile, other countries of less geopolitical importance to the United States were refused funds, even though their record in implementing IMF programmes was similar to or even better than Turkey's. Sometimes the IMF refuses immediate relief to certain countries because of corruption (as it did Kenya before the 2003 elections), but it gave $10 billion to Indonesia in November 1997 after the Asian economic crisis.

What about the future?
Shocks
It is unlikely that things will improve in the foreseeable future. In free-trade talks with Chile and Singapore in 2002, the Bush administration said that it would penalise these countries if they ever used capital controls. Jagdish Bhagwati from Columbia University and Daniel Tarullo from Georgetown University call this "a discouraging triumph of ideology over experience and good sense". In large part because there has been no real change in how financial markets behave, how the IMF behaves, how the American Treasury behaves and how hot money moves in and out of so many countries, there will be more crises in emerging markets. In such circumstances, it is most unlikely that governments will change the way they respond (or are forced to respond) when a crisis is in the offing or actually occurs.

Rebound
In most cases, markets will demonstrate their resilience and bounce back after a crisis.

Opportunity knocks despite the risks
Emerging markets are exceptionally profitable if the business approach is sound and geared towards long-term investing for sustainable profit growth.

What happens when a market collapses?
Crises happen expectedly and unexpectedly, but whichever is the case,

companies should have, at the minimum, an idea of how to react to them.

When a crisis does hit, most companies automatically engage in a strategy to "protect the bottom line" and cut fixed costs, especially staff. After all, in the developed world, it is common practice to lay off people during an economic slowdown and start hiring again when things improve. But most emerging markets bounce back fairly quickly after a crisis and radical cost-cutting can leave a company too weak to take advantage of the upturn and at the mercy of braver competitors who use the crisis to build up market share cheaply.

Russia

In early September 1998, a few weeks after the Russian rouble crash, when most western companies were cutting staff and bemoaning their losses, a Moscow-based manager of a European multinational had started to interview people for several hundred sales positions. He expressed his delight:

> This is my chance to get a better market position. All our publicly listed competitors will go through their regular knee-jerk reaction and make cuts across the board. Their bosses demand they protect the bottom line for this and the next quarter immediately. Our owners don't care about the next few quarters.

The next day a general manager in charge of Russian operations for a publicly quoted multinational said:

> I got a call last night from headquarters and the big boss said I knew what I had to do. I tried to ask if I could keep certain individuals but he interrupted and said that the budget is the most important thing at the moment.

The decision was disappointing but did not surprise him. When told about the company starting to hire during the crisis, he said: "That's what I would do if this were my company."

Most Russia-based managers of publicly listed companies that year were reluctant to implement a knee-jerk reaction from the top but had little choice. One manager said:

*When this crisis is over, and it will be over sooner than people
think [which proved correct], I will be without some great,
well-trained people and there are so many things I'll have to do
all over again. Time and money will be lost. Worse, our market
position will surely suffer.*

The Russian market started to recover less than a year later. By then,
privately held foreign companies and domestic companies had strengthened their market positions. Local companies also benefited from a
switch to cheaper local products by impoverished consumers. In these
companies, which had maintained or even increased staff numbers,
staff loyalty rose, turnover increased and market share jumped.

By contrast, those companies that had cut staff and costs did not have
the human resources needed to take advantage of new business opportunities. When they started to hire, after spending a long time convincing
headquarters it was a good idea to do so, the cost was high (as usual) and
the quality of those who applied was not as good (on average) as those they
had got rid of. Furthermore, they had acquired a reputation for not being
loyal to their staff – and reputation matters when you are trying to attract
able and qualified staff from a shallow pool of talent and experience.

Squaring the circle
Even if the pressure to cut costs cannot be avoided, companies should
consider these options.

- ◢ **Redeploy staff.** Some companies send skilled, trained executives
  to other growth markets around the world or to headquarters,
  until the crisis markets show signs of bouncing back. To enable
  this kind of movement, companies with operations in crisis-prone
  emerging markets should have a system which allows quick
  global reaction to a crisis.
- ◢ **Cut pay not staff.** Ask staff if they would take a pay cut instead
  of facing lay-offs. It is important that staff understand the
  pressure from the top and that the pay cut will last only until
  sales return to pre-crisis levels. In Russia, white-collar workers
  often approached their management with this kind of proposal
  and in many cases it was accepted. Hire and fire policies are
  culturally unacceptable in many emerging markets.
- ◢ **Cut alternatives to staff.** Look at other ways of cutting costs
  before laying off staff. Renegotiate the rent, for example, or move

to a cheaper location. Remove the hard-currency link to locally paid salaries of white-collar employees.

During crises, companies are under pressure to raise prices, but doing this to, say, negate or reduce the effect of a devaluation will not work because consumers will not be able to pay the new prices. Conversely, maintaining local prices after a devaluation is dangerous because it is likely to mean selling at a loss and it may set a precedent with regard to prices. Finding the balance is hard and varies according to the sector.

Some companies argue that crises turn out to be positive for their operations, making them lean and mean, and providing an opportunity to get rid of average and bad performers. Maybe – but at what cost? In emerging markets, it is better to hire the right people in the first place and focus on steady growth. When a crisis strikes, consider buying or acquiring local firms that have suddenly become cheaper. Or consider acquiring more land, especially if you are planning to expand manufacturing in the medium term.

Is the next crisis just around the corner?

It has been hard for institutional investors to earn decent returns in recent years. The bursting of the stockmarket bubble created a tough market for investment in equities, and returns on government bonds in safe havens have been low. To generate good returns, institutional investors have put money in more risky investments – the government bonds of many emerging markets – increasing their exposure to emerging-market risk to the highest level since the 1997 Asian crisis. In early 2004, the yield spread of emerging-market debt over American Treasuries reached its lowest level since 1998. Meanwhile, many emerging-market governments have been borrowing in hard currency because of low interest rates on the world's major currencies.

This poses two major threats to economic stability. First, institutional investors' positive sentiment towards emerging markets might reverse. If this reversal is sudden and panicky (which can be expected), the outflow of portfolio investment will destabilise some emerging-market economies. The contagion may also spread regionally and even globally. The rush to exit from what seems a bit of a bubble would be triggered by enthusiasm about investment vehicles in the developed world. Second, increases in interest rates (the first may be in the United States) in developed economies would increase the cost of debt servicing for the emerging-market economies that have increased their borrowing to unsustainable levels, hitting those with high debt burdens and no capital controls first.

2
THE OUTLOOK FOR DIFFERENT MARKETS

15 The global economy

There are only two things which are infinite. First, the universe; and second, human stupidity. But I'm not sure about the first.

Albert Einstein

This chapter aims to provide an assessment of what is going on in the global economy to help senior managers set their expectations of emerging markets at an achievable level.

The global economy is likely to pick up over the next few years in a more sluggish way than has been predicted by many. The threat for regional business managers is that optimism takes over too quickly and corporate budgets are hiked unrealistically by headquarters that are keen, as ever, to boost profits.

Factors such as hesitant corporate spending and volatile capital markets in the core OECD markets and the sluggish outlook for several years to come in Japan and Europe will have two contradictory consequences for business in emerging markets. First, corporate boards will investigate international expansion. Some will take the plunge and invest; others will decide they do not have adequate resources and position themselves in markets where they feel safer. Second, some companies will seek to square the circle by pushing for expansion in emerging markets but will not support the expansion with sufficient investment.

If senior managers are considering expansion in emerging markets, they should ensure that there is a strong business case for it and be willing to shop around. For example, what incentives will they get for investing in country A instead of country B?

Global economic factors

Predicting the future is impossible, but those involved in or contemplating investing in emerging markets should consider the following factors.

- ▱ Global growth is likely to bounce back to around 4% in the next three years or so, but risks abound and the sustainability of such growth is questionable.
- ▱ Because of the outlook in the developed world, multinationals will put more pressure on managers in emerging markets to increase profits.

▢ The pattern of global demand is unbalanced and is likely to be exacerbated by recent currency fluctuations. Total domestic demand in 2003 was 3.6% in Canada, 2.6% in the UK and the United States, 1% in the euro zone and 0.6% in Germany and Japan.

▢ Given that the average price/earnings ratio in early 2004 of American stocks was about 26, compared with a historic average since 1960 of 16, there is an argument that the Dow Industrial index should fall another 35% (from its end-2003 level). However, other factors are in play, not least fairly resilient American productivity.

▢ Although the American market will benefit from low interest rates, a low dollar and deficit spending, it could still find itself in serious trouble if budget spending is misdirected and state and city budgets are cut.

▢ If the property markets in the United States and the UK collapse, this could tip the United States into recession and destroy the UK's recent record as one of the best-performing OECD economies.

▢ EU growth will be sluggish while the German economy continues to struggle and the French and Italian economies slow down.

▢ The rigid approach of the European Central Bank will probably contribute to the economic slowdown in the EU.

▢ EU expansion offers good business opportunities in the medium term, but central and east European governments will curb spending in the next few years as they try to get their budget deficits in order.

▢ Among emerging markets, China is playing more of a pivotal role and is on the way to replacing Japan as the Asian economic powerhouse; it will, however, need at least five years to sort out its macroeconomic contradictions.

▢ Tensions in the Middle East will add to global uncertainty and limit business opportunities in the region.

▢ The threat of terrorism will continue to have a negative effect on consumer optimism, tourism, the world's major airlines and related industries.

Dollar and euro factors

▢ A weak dollar will boost American exports and corporate earnings.

- ◪ EU growth and exports will be adversely affected by a combination of a stronger euro and a weaker dollar.
- ◪ When currencies rise (as the euro has in recent times) the effect on growth and inflation will be the same as if interest rates were rising. When currencies fall (as the dollar has in recent times) the effect will be the same as if interest rates were falling. And even if the central bank has raised or cut interest rates to a certain level, the change in a currency's value may have a greater effect than the one officially intended.
- ◪ On past performance, the European Central Bank will not act sufficiently quickly or forcefully to ensure that negative effects of fluctuations in the value of the euro are not too sustained.
- ◪ The late 2003 change in American exchange-rate policy, whereby the authorities actually encouraged a fall in the dollar's value, puts a big question mark over a global economy that is already extremely fragile.

Global business growth trends

The following averages for top-line corporate growth in 2002–03 are based on what executives from major American and European consumer goods, food and beverages, chemicals and pharmaceuticals companies have reported to the authors.

Table 15.1 **Global business: estimated sales growth by region, 2002–03 (%)**

US	3
Europe	2
Japan & Germany	1
Latin America	2
Africa	2[a]
China	25
Central Europe	15
Russia	25–30

a The outlook is bleak.

Sales growth in the major developed markets and large parts of the developing world was 1–3% between 2002 and 2003 and will probably rise by a couple of percentage points in the following three years. Companies looking for dramatic increases in growth are likely to turn to mergers and acquisitions and will try to get more from emerging markets.

In order of importance, markets that are likely to provide the best growth in the next five years or so are:

◪ China;
◪ Russia;
◪ Central Europe;
◪ parts of South-East Asia (South Korea);
◪ South Africa (possibly);
◪ Turkey (possibly);
◪ Iran (possibly and eventually);
◪ Dubai.

Although senior managers have focused more on corporate branding, corporate governance and corporate social responsibility, there has also been the start of a move away from global product lines and a return to regionalism in market segmentation. This applies especially to the way big multinational companies are addressing emerging markets. It seems that, even if they are not moving to fully fledged regionalism, markets by region are at least getting more attention.

How investors look at emerging markets

Not surprisingly, portfolio investors move quickly in and out of emerging markets and tend to follow the herd (see Chapter 14). They often form part of the crisis in these markets: Mexico in the 1980s, Asia in 1997 and Russia in 1998. According to the Institute of International Finance, net private capital flows to emerging markets leapt from $40 billion in 1990 to $330 billion in 1996, but then fell sharply to $145 billion in 1998. They climbed back to $190 billion in 2000 as developed countries' confidence grew and Asia, central Europe and parts of Latin America prospered. However, as concerns about Argentina and Brazil mounted and global confidence sagged, capital flows fell again in 2002 to $115 billion. In 2003, they rose to about $140 billion.

In emerging markets, foreign direct investment (FDI) generally "sticks" more than the portfolio variety because it is much more difficult to close down a factory than it is to sell a few bonds. FDI in emerging markets rose in the early and mid-1990s (see Table 15.2) and maintained steady levels even in the wake of the Asian and Russian financial crashes of 1997–98. It seems that confidence about the strength of home markets and the global economy outweighed any doubts about emerging markets. Only in 2001 did FDI in emerging markets start to fall. This was largely the result of a global collapse in confidence, and because, as privatisation programmes came to an end in certain regions, there were fewer juicy investment opportunities. There was also a big drop in investment in Latin America.

Table 15.2 **FDI flows into emerging markets ($bn)**

1993	1995	1997	1998	1999	2000	2001	2002	2003ᵃ
85	128	208	216	251	266	228	204	227

a Estimate.
Source: Economist Intelligence Unit

One attractive region for FDI inflows in recent years has been central and eastern Europe. For example, in 2002, when overall FDI to emerging markets fell by some 10%, FDI into central and eastern Europe rose by almost 20% from $27 billion to $32 billion. This was a year when FDI into many developed markets collapsed, falling by, for example, 77% in the United States, 60% in the UK and 24% in Spain. Most of the investment in central and eastern Europe is now in greenfield projects as the major privatisation programmes have ended. Within the region, the Czech Republic and Poland remain the two largest recipients, but Russia, starting from a low base, is likely to take over in 2004 as the regional leader as a result of investments in the oil sector by BP and Shell, among others. As Russian opportunities grew, FDI in central and eastern Europe fell to $19 billion in 2003, compared with $23 billion the previous year. Investment in Hungary and Slovakia was particularly slow.

Overall, foreign direct investors – at least those who have already invested – take a longer-term view of the markets. Some of those planning to invest in emerging markets take an unrealistically short-term view of returns and therefore do not invest in the first place or get frustrated with the rate of return when the investment has been made. Some regional managers complain that "headquarters want to recoup the entire investment in three years". According to a manager of an American auto company:

We had to work like hell to convince senior management to
give us a return on investment period of seven years.

Peter Brabeck, CEO of Nestlé, has said that you cannot treat emerging markets as you do developed ones. He notes that emerging markets such as Russia and China require 5–10 years and that during that time any emerging market can undergo financial or economic turmoil or collapse. Companies that want to succeed in emerging markets need more patience and stamina. Nestlé lost money for ten years in South Korea and China, but it persisted and now both operations are highly profitable. The company also persisted in Russia after the 1998 rouble crash and over the following 18 months doubled its market share in key product segments. That Nestlé chooses not to be fully quoted in the United States (where its shares can only be purchased via American depositary receipts or ADRs) has made it easier for the company to take a long-term view.

Many emerging markets have the same features: they often provide good growth, but individually can be small in both the volume of business and the amount of profit they add to a global company's bottom line. As a senior manager of a leading American pharmaceuticals company notes:

90% of our profits are in Europe, the US and Japan. The rest of
the world is immense in size but peanuts for the business.

This is certainly true for pharmaceuticals companies, but some emerging markets, such as Russia, Brazil and Turkey, can also be highly profitable when business is going well. Moreover, markets such as China are beginning to have a noticeable impact on the global profits of multinational companies. So far, emerging markets have been the icing on the cake but just as sweet for that. This is why, as the global economy slows, more companies are looking at some of the larger developing markets, particularly China and Russia (see Chapters 16 and 17).

Many consumer goods, food and beverages, and pharmaceuticals companies have reported good profits in emerging markets, particularly in central Europe and Russia. In the latter, until recently, most companies could charge premium prices for their products. Most western pharmaceuticals companies charge 20–35% more for their products in central Europe than they do in Spain, attributing the need for higher prices to the risks of an underdeveloped distribution system.

According to a manager of one of the world's largest packaging companies, "Brazil and Russia are our two most profitable markets in the world." The European finance manager of one of the largest American consumer goods companies rated his company's profit margins in different regions as follows:

> In the West we aim for and achieve an average profit margin of 6–7%. In central Europe we aim for and achieve 9–14%. In Russia we aim for and achieve 17–20%.

The figures in Table 15.2 on page 135 indicate that interest in emerging markets has remained firm during the economic downturn. The increase of some 10% in 2003 compared with a year earlier shows continued and increasing interest, and many of the decisions for those investments would have been planned in 2001–02.

Some companies adopt a middle strategy, saying, "let's look at emerging markets more, and look to export more to them, but hold back from on-the-ground investment in plant and production as it is too risky". In most companies, investment in new assets requires jumping over more hurdles to get approval to go ahead. As a regional manager of an American consumer goods company notes:

> If I need $20m for marketing purposes in emerging markets, that's fine, but if we ask to invest the same amount in assets or production facilities, then senior management goes crazy. We need to spend about three years in internal debates and sign off on 500 internal documents.

The mixed picture is understandable as some emerging markets can prove highly profitable. Given their diverse geography and politics, it is inevitable that something is going wrong in some emerging markets at any time. Most markets in Africa have been generally poor for 5–10 years and many of those in the Middle East for some 2–3 years. Asian markets have fluctuated in their recovery from the 1997 crash. Until recently, financial markets have not differentiated between emerging markets; when one went belly up, they pulled back from them all.

The trick is to pick the winners and losers in the emerging markets, sometimes on the basis of the instinct of regional managers, and to show commitment to these decisions before they bear fruit, often over a longer time frame than in developed markets.

The global oil price outlook

The oil price has an important effect on the costs of companies globally and on the revenues of many emerging markets. Most commentators argue that the oil price ($27–29 per barrel in early 2004) will fall in the coming years. This is possible, but the fall may be delayed another year or so by the following factors.

◪ OPEC (Organisation of the Petroleum Exporting Countries) will try hard to maintain discipline in quotas to keep the price at about $23–25 per barrel, even though it may not quite succeed in sticking to this target.)

◪ Russian companies are less likely to engage in a market share war, which was what caused prices to fall in 2002.

◪ Bringing Iraqi oil back on stream will take a couple of years.

◪ Demand for oil in China will rise significantly (the country became a net oil importer in 1993) and American demand is expected to rise by 25% in the next 15 years.

However, there are several good reasons to suggest that the oil price will start to fall after 2004.

◪ Global demand will be at best steady.

◪ Venezuelan oil streams will probably grow in 2004.

◪ New oilfields and pipelines (such as in Azerbaijan, Canada and Kazakhstan) will ensure more volume from non-OPEC sources.

◪ Iraqi oil will start to come back on stream in 2004 and reach a higher capacity in 2005–06.

Predicting the oil price is a mug's game, but it is likely that the oil price will fall over 2004–08 though possibly not as suddenly as other commentators reckon. The longer-term outlook is hazier. By 2013 the world will be consuming 20% more oil than it does today, involving a rise in consumption from 77m barrels per day to 90m barrels per day in ten years. This too need not entail a sharp price hike, as by then Iraqi oilfields, along with other new ones, will be fully on stream.

Table 15.3 **GDP growth based on a middle-case global scenario, 2000–07 (%)**

	2000	2001	2002	2003	2004	2005	2006	2007
World[a]	4.5	2.1	2.7	2.8	3.5	3.9	4.2	3.9
United States	3.8	0.3	2.4	2.2	3.2	3.2	3.1	3.0
Euro zone	3.7	1.4	0.7	0.7	1.6	2.2	2.1	2.4
Japan	2.1	−0.5	−0.5	0.5	0.6	1.0	1.2	1.0
Asia & Australasia	4.1	1.8	2.7	3.1	3.3	3.5	3.6	3.7
Latin America	3.8	0.2	−0.9	1.8	3.1	3.3	3.4	3.7
Middle East & North Africa	4.6	2.0	1.3	2.7	3.8	4.1	4.1	4.3
Sub-Saharan Africa	3.3	2.7	2.6	3.1	3.8	3.4	3.3	3.2
CEE & CIS[b]	6.7	4.4	3.4	4.5	4.3	4.1	4.0	4.5

Note: 2000–02 figures are actual; 2003–07 figures are estimates.
a At purchasing power parity.
b Central and eastern Europe and Commonwealth of Independent States (this includes most of the former Soviet Union).
Source: Daniel Thorniley

The American economy

The current downturn is the worst I have experienced.

Larry Ellison, chairman of Oracle, in 2002

What makes this economic downturn unusual is that all three major economies – Japan, western Europe and the United States – are in difficulty. In the past at least one of them was on the up when one or both of the others were struggling. As a result, the slowdown will last longer and growth is likely to remain below potential for the next five years for the three major economies (especially Japan).

The United States has done better than the others because of a falling dollar, low real interest rates and budget deficit spending. This is why the American economy will grow by at least one percentage point more than Europe's and two percentage points more than Japan's. Nevertheless, there were mixed messages about American corporate earnings and profits in 2003, when more than 80% of all earnings growth was coming from cost cuttings. The United States is still dependent on consumer spending and government fiscal policy, and any recovery will be slow.

American consumers, together with maintained levels of productivity in the economy (which is remarkable in such a period of decline), have been the lifesavers of the American economy. But it is the credit-fuelled house-price boom that has helped sustain consumer spending. Individual stockholders lost about £3 trillion in the stockmarket fall, but recouped about $1.5 trillion because of the higher prices of their houses. As a result, in 2002, when American incomes rose by 2%, borrowing rose by 10% as consumers used the paper capital gains on their houses as collateral. If the property market goes into decline, there could be a sharp downturn in consumer confidence.

The Federal Reserve has taken an active approach to managing the downturn with numerous interest-rate cuts, but in May 2003, with core inflation down to 1.5%, the lowest since John F. Kennedy was president, Alan Greenspan, the boss of the Fed, highlighted the threats to the American economy of deflation. For the first time in 40 years, the Fed does not want inflation to be any lower.

While inflation was the bad boy of the American economy, a strong dollar helped keep down inflation pressures by making foreign imports look cheap in the domestic market; in other words, foreign inflation was not being imported. But the strong dollar also made the trade deficit and the current account worse (the worst in absolute and percentage terms since 1776), the latter running at record levels of almost $525 billion and over 5% of GDP in 2003. And it made American exports more expensive.

In the past the policy on the current-account deficit was relaxed. The strong dollar ensured that foreign investors were happy to provide the needed daily net investment of $1.5 billion because they got good returns on a strong currency. But the downturn in the stockmarket opened up the possibility that the global appetite for American assets could possibly waver, which meant that a blind eye could no longer be turned to the current-account deficit.

All the better then that the policy to combat deflation entails a falling dollar, as this would not only help fight deflation but would also curb the trade and current-account deficits. Thus the Fed is able to kill at least two birds with one stone – although it usually takes a year or two for a fall in a currency to have much of an impact on the current-account deficit.

The theory is that a sliding currency will combat deflation, boost exports, instil inflationary expectations and allow companies to raise prices and hence boost profits and wages. In practice, however, the dollar could fall in value too much. After all, it has been rising in value too much in recent years. Most commentators and economists have argued that on a purchasing-power parity basis the euro is overvalued when it exceeds $1.12: this view is likely to hold for the next few years.

No doubt Greenspan would love to be able to say something to the effect that: "We'll have the dollar at €1.17 for five months and then have it at €1.27 for two months and then have the rate come down to €1.12 for another six months and then let it settle at €1.08 for a couple of years." Alas, he and we know that such rational fine-tuning on the financial markets is impossible.

Another technical destabiliser is the hedging of the dollar by European companies. Since this involves selling the dollar forward, the risk of a vicious circle grows as the currency falls further.

What is the danger of a profound overshooting? If the dollar plummets to €1.30-1.50 or more for a sustained period (despite the purchasing of American assets by Asian central banks in an effort to prevent their currencies strengthening), the Fed will find itself not facing the danger of deflation but instead that of quickly rising inflation. It would be obliged to raise rates quickly, when the real economy was only just recovering, setting off another economic downturn.

Although the benefits to the American economy of a falling dollar and low interest rates are clear, they are less so in the case of the policy of tax cuts. Tax cuts can help the economy by putting more cash in people's pockets, but it depends on whose pockets and what they intend to do with the money. Nor is it proven that tax cuts are an automatic driver in creating jobs.

Note also that because the federal government has imposed more spending requirements on them without providing the finance to meet those requirements, state and local governments throughout most of the country had to slash spending and benefits as they, unlike the federal government, are not allowed legally to run deficits. This could counteract the economic stimulus effect that may stem from the federal tax cut package introduced by the Bush administration in 2002.

In short, the worst-case scenario is that the tax cut package does not provide an economic stimulus, tax revenues fall and the deficit rises along with long-term interest rates. This will result in higher borrowing costs, which will impede business investment and job creation.

Whatever happens, it is clearly unwise to assume that the American economy is "bound" to bounce back quickly – and when the economy is struggling American companies are less inclined to invest in emerging markets. An American downturn will keep many economies across the world, from Latin America to Asia to Europe, in a weaker position because there will be less trading with the United States.

Euro zone

The outlook for the euro zone is sober. Germany is the big worry, with the prospect of sluggish growth continuing beyond the mid-2000s and more deflationary pressures. Most managers working in Germany feel that business is in for a tough time in the next few years. After the reconstruction boom of the early 1990s, German GDP growth has lagged behind that of the rest of the euro zone: since 1996 it has averaged 1.6% a year compared with 2.5% for the euro zone. The consensus for 2003 was that Germany would struggle to achieve 1% growth, compared with 1.4% in the euro zone and 2.6% in the United States.

The country's current problems include the following.

◪ Slowing retail sales and domestic demand. Consumption contracted in six out of the eight quarters of 2002–03. Germans have been choosing to save their money rather than spend it, and weaker growth of disposable income has been reinforcing this trend. Unlike Americans and Britons, Germans have not been engaging in mortgage equity withdrawal and the shallow property market is stagnant.

◪ Hourly wage costs in 2004 remained high in west Germany: 13% higher than in the United States, 43% more than in the UK and 60% more than in Spain. Germany's once strong productivity no longer compensates as much for these costs. Since the mid-1990s, social security costs have risen 2.5 times faster than GDP.

◪ Unemployment in 2004 seemed stuck at over 4m (10%).

◪ As a consequence of slower growth and higher unemployment, tax revenue has been falling, worsening the budget deficit.

◪ Among OECD countries, Germany's stockmarket fell the most by far in 2002 because of the weakness of the economy and the market's dependence on the financial sector (33% of the market) and the IT sector (10%).

◪ The banking sector is fragile and Germany is "over-banked" – there are more bank branches than butchers' shops. More bank mergers are on the way. Medium-sized German companies (*Mittelstand*) rely more on borrowing than on raising equity; so when they go bust, as many have, the banking sector is hurt proportionately more than in other countries. Banks then rein in their lending and the *Mittelstand* struggle to survive. Banks' capital ratios (the amount of reserves they hold and are expected to hold) are already low. (The lower the ratio, the more vulnerable banks are to economic downturns and corporate bankruptcies.) Provisions for bad debt pushed all four major banks into losses in 2002. The sector's debt structure is vulnerable to deflation.

◾ The stronger euro will hinder European and German exports. Germany's share of global exports has already fallen from 12% in 1992 to 10% in 2002. Estimates suggest that for every 10% of euro appreciation, euro zone growth is reduced by 1%.

Reforms in labour markets, tax and pensions will be implemented over time. But Germany missed a chance in 1999–2000 when growth was marginally stronger and the economy was in better shape to absorb the shocks of reform (as could also be said of France). Is now the appropriate time for Germany to undertake a deep restructuring of its economy and social policies? Some would say yes, the bitter medicine must be swallowed. But it would plunge Germany and Europe into recession at a time of volatile global markets and already weak business confidence. This would have a further negative impact on emerging markets dependent on exporting to the EU.

Another problem is that Germans do not want reform, especially of their labour laws and pensions or of the other state benefits they currently receive. Neither main political party was keen to introduce reforms before or after the 2002 elections. Consequently, any reforms are likely to be implemented slowly.

With Germany embarking on public spending cuts and budget tightening measures, and France and Italy close to breaking budget deficit targets, the chances of sharply lower growth in the euro zone are high. Euro zone growth is likely to be at least one percentage point less than US growth for several years. Corporate investment is likely to be slow to pick up, and if the euro remains strong, exports will be hit. In economies with low savings ratios, there will be more saving and less spending as it dawns on most citizens aged over 40 that they have no realistic chance of a decent pension when they retire.

Weakness in the job market and poor consumer confidence will undermine any positive trends in real wages (for example, in France). Tax incentives, both corporate and personal, in Italy and France are having a limited impact on domestic demand and capital investment against a background of low consumer and corporate confidence. The threat of deflation looms. EU expansion offers good business opportunities in the medium term, but the new member states will have to curb spending in the next few years as they try to control their budget deficits.

The change in American exchange-rate policy, allowing the dollar to fall substantially against the euro, puts a new big question mark over an already fragile global economy. The weak dollar will help American firms sell more abroad and US corporate earnings will benefit. But European growth and exports will be badly hit. The European Central Bank (ECB) will have to act quickly and forcefully to ensure the negative impacts of a weaker dollar are not too sustained. It will probably fail to do so.

Estimates suggest that a 5% increase in the value of the euro has the same impact on the European economy as a 1% increase in interest rates has on inflation and growth. In other words, in 2003 the ECB's 0.75% rate cuts did little to compensate for a 6% rise in the value of the euro. It is as if the euro economy spent the year with rising interest rates at a time when many commentators felt that the ECB current nominal rate of 2% was at least 1% too high for the German economy.

In 2003 some 30% of German goods and services used to calculate the consumer price index showed falling prices; in 2002 German retail sales fell 2.5% compared with 2001. German consumers are demanding lower prices, with the result that 30% of the retail market is supplied by discounts. They are beginning to get the Japanese habit of sitting on their money waiting for falling prices.

The German economy is (or was) Europe's engine; trends in Germany, France and Italy are the ones that really matter for Europe as a whole. The ECB should now pay less attention to inflation (which is currently only a potential problem in such countries as Spain, Portugal, Ireland and Greece) and focus more on deflation in the major economies.

As the euro rises, inflation will fall and growth will slow. Deflation is threatening. In 2003 the core inflation rate in Germany was 0.6%. Estimates for France suggest an inflation rate of 0% by the end of 2004. On current trends of growth and exchange rate, core inflation in 2004–05 could be as low as 0.7% in the whole of the EU.

Major exporting companies such as Henkel and Siemens are already predicting reduced corporate earnings on account of the rising euro. Henkel's share price has already been hit as it predicts slower 2003 sales. On average and across sectors, the top 500 European companies obtain 20% of their revenue from exports to or sales in the United States. This is hardly surprisingly given that $350 billion of the $700 billion invested in the American economy in the four years 1997–2000 came from European investors. So the falling dollar is bound to have an impact on European corporate results. Estimates suggest that a 10% rise in the euro takes 4% off average European corporate earnings growth.

Of course, multinational companies can hedge against this and do so. But Volkswagen reported first quarter 2003 earnings that were €400m less than expected as its hedging programme covered only 40% of American revenues. Big players such as BMW benefit from natural hedges, in that more than 50% of their sales stem from non-euro markets and a lot of production costs are taken locally, thereby reducing currency risks.

Complaints that the EU's economy is poor and structural reforms are needed in labour and product markets miss the point. Such reforms, even if they are approved, will take years to have an impact and any benefits will arrive too late. The priority now is to get monetary policy in line with the needs of the economy and to face the threat of deflation. Monetary policy also takes time (at least a year) to have an effect, but it works more quickly than structural reforms. A forceful monetary response acknowledging the threat of deflation would also send an appropriate signal to the markets and to consumers.

Europe needs a looser monetary policy, a more flexible fiscal policy and structural reforms. At the moment it has none of these. If steps are not taken, in a few years Europe may look like Germany does today.

The ECB and the Growth and Stability Pact need a thorough overhaul. The ECB's monetary policy and the outmoded 3% budget deficit ceiling explain in large part why Germany is struggling and cannot resort to standard anti-recession policies. Romano Prodi, president of the European Commission, has called the pact "stupid" and the trade commissioner has called it "medieval", but reform will not take place soon. The danger is that without at least "time out" on the straitjacket of the Growth and Stability Pact and if it slips into deflation, Europe could find itself gripped by a severe recession for which the standard remedies may not be enough.

Japan

Japan's economy hit the doldrums back in 1990–91, and the policy response to its woes has been unsure and ineffective. Pump-priming and zero interest rates have failed because heavily indebted companies do not want to borrow and banks overflowing with bad loans do not want to lend. Base money (currency plus demand deposits) in the banks has soared, but consumers choose not to take out the money and spend it. The government spending splurge has done nothing but drive domestic debt to 140% of GDP and the budget deficit to 8%, both the worst in the OECD; much of the budget deficit stems from falling tax revenues. Unemployment in the country previously known for its culture of "jobs for life" has soared, and the stockmarket has plunged. The commercial property market is 80% lower than its peak in 1989. Growth was negative in 2002 (-0.5%), negative/flat in 2003 and will barely exceed 1% for the next few years. At the end of 2003 deflation was intensifying, consumer confidence and retail sales were decreasing, wages had been falling by 1% a year, exports were flagging and the biggest banks were sitting on ¥5 trillion ($42 billion) of paper losses on equity holdings.

The country will need at least five years to sort out its macroeconomic contradictions. (A joke going around in 2003 was: Question: what's the difference between Argentina and Japan? Answer: five years.) Japan's failure to take effective action to combat inflation raises concern that the economic situation could get worse and even spread, affecting in particular Asian developing countries but also other parts of the world.

The outlook for Japan is not good. What is needed is a mixture of bank reform, corporate restructuring and monetary loosening, to enable the Bank of Japan to buy back government debt and even some American treasuries in order to bring down the value of the yen and to increase inflation (the bogeyman of the 1970s).

A 2002 OECD report urged the authorities to adopt a two-pronged approach of monetary loosening and to move into uncharted territories by purchasing more government bonds and setting an inflation target, and by implication printing more money to boost inflation. The OECD also stated:

> There is no alternative to revitalising the economy through structural reform and there is no more time to be wasted.

Even with reform and a possible shift in monetary policy, one underlying feature that will not go away is the corruption that has coloured politics and business in Japan since the late 1950s, as evidenced in 2002 by the assassination of Koki Ishii, for 40 years a parliamentarian and an outspoken critic of corruption in the government and the construction industry.

Japan's GDP did pick up in 2003 as a result of an increase in exports (70% of which headed to China) and improvements in some larger Japanese companies, which managed to reduce debt. But it remains to be seen whether this recovery is sustainable.

The deflation threat

Globalisation, intense competition and tougher anti-monopoly legislation have intensified the trend of falling prices.

Deflation can result when economies are operating below trend, when there is a gap between actual and potential output. The OECD reckoned that every G7 country with the exception of Canada would have an output gap in 2003 leading to falling inflation but not necessarily deflation (a persistent fall in the overall price level). It also estimated that the American economy would grow at about 1% below its trend rate of 3%. If American growth continues below trend, prices will continue to fall and inflation will become negative in 2–3 years. The outlook is essentially the same for the euro zone.

Inflation and growth trends do not have to go in the same direction. If the level of GDP is below potential, inflation can fall and continue to fall, even when an economy is growing, against a backdrop of rising spare capacity (which can only be filled by higher growth).

Deflation is harder to get rid of than inflation and can be more damaging because:

- wages normally fall more slowly than prices and thus corporate profits fall;
- consumers delay spending in anticipation of prices falling further;
- against this background, companies are unable (or at least less able) to pass on price rises;
- overall investment falls;
- bankruptcies increase and companies go bust;
- unemployment rises and consumers cut their spending;
- the growth rate falls;
- as debtors go bust, banks become more reluctant to lend and more ready to foreclose on debtors in order to get at least some of their money back;
- central banks' monetary-policy weapons become blunter – and once rates hit zero (as in Japan), they cannot offer negative real interest rates;
- the real burden of debt swells as prices fall. Debtors often cut their investments and sell assets in a spiral of declining asset and income values, suppressing growth and increasing unemployment.

16 The business outlook

This chapter examines current and future business trends and issues in some of the major emerging markets, focusing on countries with the best potential in the next few years.

Emerging markets became increasingly popular places to invest during the 1990s as foreign direct investment (FDI) flows more than tripled between 1993 and 2000 (see Table 15.2 on page 135). Even after the global economy slowed in 2001, investment in emerging markets as a whole remained steady and grew strongly in, for example, China and central and eastern Europe. The anecdotal evidence from CEOs and regional managers is that the number of companies seriously considering expanding their business in emerging markets is growing.

Emerging markets enjoy mixed fortunes. Some can prove very profitable, but they are never all doing well at the same time. Given their diverse geography and politics, it is inevitable that at any particular time something is going wrong in some of them. The trick for investors is to pick the winners and avoid losers.

Central and eastern Europe

Against a sombre global outlook, central and eastern Europe and Russia are reporting solid results compared with other emerging markets and developed ones. This has led companies to pay much more attention to the region. However, the danger is that companies which already have a presence there will expect too high a return from the region.

The CEE/CIS region has outperformed all other emerging-market regions since 2000 and is likely to do so for the rest of the decade (see Table 16.1). Even if there was global economic crisis (civil war in Argentina, military takeover in Turkey, conflict between India and Pakistan), the CEE region would come out of it reasonably well and better than other regions. (This is not to stay that the region would be left undamaged commercially, only that the pain would be less, perhaps a lot less.)

An analogy with boxing helps explain why. Several heavyweight fighters in recent years have entered the ring when they were well past their prime. They were overweight but their layers of fat let them absorb many punches and come away with a substantial amount of money. In the same way, the CEE region has the following elements that help protect it.

- **Strong GDP growth.** CEE growth is falling, hit by the downturn in Germany, the region's main export debt nation, and by the global slowdown. But it is falling from higher levels than in any other region and has more resources to fall back on.
- **Underlying strong currencies.** Nearly all the major CEE currencies have appreciated strongly over the past few years, giving them a cushion for times of weakness. The main currency factor over the next few years will be euro entry, tentatively scheduled for 2009: most CEE governments will want to ensure that their currencies adopt a rate for conversion to the euro before entry which is low enough to ensure that the euro does not destroy growth. So although the currencies in the CEE region are likely to fall, with the exception of Hungary perhaps, this does not necessarily point to underlying economic weakness.
- **Political stability.** Politics have become "normal" in central Europe. The risks for weak governments are, as in the developed world, of early elections, not coups or terrorist attacks. "There are not many al-Qaeda networks in Budapest," said one executive.
- **The EU as a guarantor.** The prospect and reality of EU membership boosts growth prospects in the region by anchoring reform and stability, and providing the right climate for increased trade and investment.
- **Falling inflation.** A few years ago double-digit inflation seemed entrenched, but now the outlook for the core CEE markets (Czech Republic, Hungary, Poland and Slovakia) is for sustained lower inflation as EU convergence continues. This is not to say that inflation will not "bounce around", and certainly there is potential for a rise in Poland, the Czech Republic and Slovakia, but any upward move would not be sustained and comes in any case from historic lows.
- **Rising labour productivity.** Higher growth and falling inflation are largely the result of rising labour productivity in many markets because of tight fiscal and monetary policies and the impact of technology and FDI in several economies.
- **Improving banking sector.** Weak financial sectors are the Achilles heel of many emerging markets and have caused severe problems in most of central Europe too over the past ten years. But most of the banking sector (over 90% in most countries) has now been acquired by western financial institutions, which will

soon want to expand rapidly their lending to CEE corporations and citizens. This will stimulate domestic demand and raise personal and corporate debt levels. In 2003, western owners of local banks were still reluctant to boost domestic commercial borrowing and were conservative in lending to local industry and local investors, much to the chagrin of the multinationals that want to do business with these locals. But things will get better in the next few years and the "banking risk" in the region has largely evaporated.

Although the CEE region is doing well, this is not always reflected in corporate results. The region has its winners and its losers, and several markets are sluggish. Furthermore, it is important to bear in mind that the region accounts for only 4% of global GDP, a figure that will rise to only 5–6% over the next 15 years (Latin America accounts for 10% of global GDP and Asia Pacific for 26%).

One manager in the consumer goods sector said:

> We are doing very well overall. Hungary is particularly strong for us. In fact we have wrapped up 4m customers in that market out of 10m and there is not much more we can do with our existing products and prices. The long-term challenge for us and others is to get to that poorer, more rural 6m customers. It will require a big shift in our marketing and I'm not sure we are up to it, nor our western competitors.

These comments are relevant also to Poland and the Czech Republic. Often individual markets for a multinational company can be broken down into the capital city and perhaps one or two other population centres. As one European telecoms vice-president noted: "Warsaw is a market within a market." The challenge and the real remaining growth potential in the core CEE markets will come increasingly from relatively untapped subregions within each of the more prosperous markets.

A regional manager of a European industrial company notes that although there is still good organic and geographic sales growth to achieve in the region, another method to obtain good returns is to go deeper into the existing customer base:

> We are selling well to them but we should now expand the portfolio of products we sell to these existing customers and

Table 16.1 **Sales growth of western companies in central and eastern Europe[a]**
2001–06 (%)

	2001	2002	2003	2004	2005	2006
Manufacturing & industrial	21	15	10–12	8	12	14
Food & beverages	22	12	8–10	7	9	10
Consumer goods	25	17	13	12	12	13
Information technology	11	13	9	7	10	13
Pharmaceuticals & health care	20	16	14	10	9	8
Over-the-counter pharmaceuticals	35	30	24	15	16	15

a Organic sales growth in core CEE markets, south-east Europe, Russia and Ukraine.
Source: 2001–03 figures are based on corporate anecdotes and surveys by the Economist Corporate Network, Vienna; 2004–06 figures are authors' estimates.

offer increasingly higher-value products ... which I'm pleased to say they are pushing for in any case.

The message is clear and sensible: aim to get more money from new clients and more money from existing ones in a maturing market. And there is still more potential out there, even as competition builds up. A regional manager of one of the world's large IT companies notes:

We have an excellent existing business and the outlook for 2004–08 is very good too. Piracy issues are improving in a couple of markets and helping top-line growth. But there is still space in the markets to grow. If I tackle Poland (ie put more investments in, increase headcount) I can probably double my existing business. And if I tackle Russia, I can quadruple my existing business.

The impact of EU enlargement on business in central and eastern Europe

It has been estimated that EU membership will add an extra half to three-quarters of a percentage point a year to the GDP of the entrant economies in 2004–08.

Table 16.2 **Countries scheduled to join the EU**

2004 (May 1st)	Czech Republic, Cyprus, Estonia, Hungary, Latvia, Lithuania, Malta, Poland, Slovenia, Slovakia
2007	Bulgaria, Romania and possibly Croatia
2010–14	Possibly Turkey

The benefits for business are significant.

◪ There will be more legal and tax transparency.
◪ The risk assessment for the region is falling and this will continue, entailing savings in financing and insurance.
◪ Many import tariffs will disappear, making western products more affordable.
◪ Customs problems will largely be eradicated, but poor infrastructure will continue to make just-in-time deliveries difficult.

For the first 5–10 years, it is likely that the rich will become richer and the poor will become poorer as the IT, financial and services sectors do well but mining, agriculture and heavy industry are restructured. The same applies to local CEE companies: the least competitive companies will fail but the more competitive ones will seek to expand their existing business in the region and to enter markets in western Europe. Western companies will face growing competition in their home markets in 2004–07.

EU enlargement will change the shape of European business, and the process has already started. Extremely low-cost production will continue to move out of CEE to cheaper labour-cost markets in Asia. But new investment is moving from western to central Europe. Western companies with production facilities in the CEE region will seek to consolidate or restructure them. A regional production plan that made sense in 1999 may need an overhaul in 2004–06. Some countries, such as Spain, may become large exporters of FDI, investing in the less-developed market to the east.

Many western companies are reassessing their CEE business portfolio, asking such questions as: What do we export? How many staff do we have, how many representative offices, how many legal entities, how many production sites? Are they adequate? Should we invest more? Western and CEE companies will consider partnerships and alliances in Europe. There will also be an increase in mergers and acquisitions as companies fight for market leadership. Those entering the market late will pay higher prices for acquisitions as all the blue-chip players were bought long ago or are fiercely independent.

Labour costs will remain low for many years. It is estimated that average wage costs in CEE will not catch up with current levels in Spain, Portugal and Greece for at least 12–15 years. This makes the CEE markets attractive as a low-cost production location within Europe. Costs for managers, office staff and technically skilled staff have already risen, and this trend will continue. Some companies will consider bringing back expatriates on short-term contracts to fill key posts as wage costs for local middle managers approach those of expatriates.

Western companies will look at their corporate structures in 2004–06. Many are establishing clusters of small CEE markets – for example, the Czech Republic and Slovakia together (again), and Hungary and Romania – or three or four markets together to make them look bigger and to give them critical mass in the European structure. The plan is to retain this structure through 2004–07 and then to modify if necessary, perhaps in 2007–09 as the countries join the euro zone.

Depending on political decisions, the political complexion of individual governments and how they fare in reducing their budget deficits, most if not all of the CEE entrants will have adopted the euro by 2010.

Senior managers in some companies are already noting that GDP in Spain and Portugal boomed after EU entry. The argument from headquarters is something like this: "You have set annual growth targets in your five-year plan for CEE of 13%, but look at what happened in Spain after it joined the EU. GDP boomed. Your targets are too low and we want you to raise your growth figure to 23%."

Fortunately, there are counters to this suggestion. First, the Cohesion countries (Spain, Portugal, Ireland and Greece) had experienced sluggish or poor growth before EU entry, so GDP jumped high from a low base. This is not the case with CEE, which has recorded good growth in recent years. The region has already benefited from EU free-trade agreements and much higher levels of foreign investment, so it will do well and GDP will benefit, but the jump will not be as high because the CEE markets will enter with a much higher starting point. Second, the EU is being less generous with its funding. Third, CEE entrants will face extra budgetary pressure because of membership fees, co-financing requirements for EU funds and the costs of implementing strict EU standards. At the same time, most will be trying to bring their budget deficits down from high levels in order to adopt the euro. Governments will have to raise excise taxes and social insurance costs, cut spending or borrow more. Consumers will have less disposable income as they pay more in taxes and social costs. But eventually the funds will flow and the overall "cake" of these economies will grow along with government and consumer spending.

Why things are getting tougher in central and eastern Europe

- **GDP growth.** Although the regional growth rate is better than all other regions in the world, many CEE markets are experiencing a slowdown in growth.
- **Competition.** Since 2002 competition has increased sharply and will continue to do so. Poland is for many companies, including Nestlé and Unilever, the most competitive market in Europe and for some the most competitive globally. The price wars being fought will shape the market for the next 5–10 years.

  In several CEE markets in 2003 there were a dozen or so western and domestic players in any product sector. This number will decrease dramatically as the market leaders assert their positions and other players are marginalised, take up niche positions or leave the market.
- **Market structure.** The structure of the market is changing and companies have to adapt. Many industrial companies have already captured the key customers, and fast-moving consumer goods companies have tackled the capital cities and one or two rich regions. Now the challenge is to extend sales into rural regions where people's disposable income is lower, a process that will challenge the marketing strategies of western multinationals.
- **Retailing.** Retailers have flooded into CEE markets and oversupplied Poland and the Czech Republic. In earlier years they went for growth and market share, whereas now they need high margins or it will be unprofitable to stay in the market. This is putting the squeeze on western consumer goods companies whose products they sell.
- **Cyclical problems.** There are usually one or two markets going through cyclical crises at any time. In 2000–03 it was Poland's turn, and the Czech Republic and Hungary each experienced a 2–3 year economic decline in the 1990s. Regional managers in most emerging market regions invariably have a mixed portfolio of several small markets, of which at least one is likely to be experiencing cyclical problems.
- **Western Europe.** Slow growth in Germany and other west European countries will affect demand for exports from the CEE region. Germany, for example, takes 31% of Czech exports.
- **Budget deficits.** This is potentially a big problem. Most of the main CEE markets are running budget deficits well over euro entry targets. Cutting the deficits will mean spending cuts or

tax increases and probably combinations of both. As governments cut spending, western companies selling to the government or its agencies, in particular pharmaceuticals, health care and IT companies, will face a tougher sales environment, and taxes and excise duties on tobacco and alcoholic beverages will rise. More taxation will take money out of consumers' pockets and lessen their discretionary spending.

How will companies respond to this? By expanding in other emerging markets such as Russia, Ukraine, south-east Europe, Turkey and South Africa and, of course, by cutting costs. A number of companies working in central and eastern Europe note that in order to keep up margins, costs are being cut against a background of slower sales.

South-east Europe

Healthy sales and profit margins are being reported by a growing number of companies in south-east Europe. Sales in Croatia are bolstered by tourism receipts, a large grey economy and a stable inflation and currency outlook. Serbia, although small in absolute terms, has grown noticeably for several years, and most people expect it to be a sizeable and important regional market in the next five years. The recently created free-trade zone for south-east Europe should boost sales, and the prospect of EU accession will sustain corporate interest. But these markets will become more competitive in 2–5 years, as is beginning to happen in Romania.

Russia

Sales growth and profit margins are still extremely good in Russia and there should be sustainable growth over the next five years. As one industrial investor put it: "Russia offers great potential for acceptable risks when the rest of the world is down."

Following the collapse of the rouble in 1998, the huge Russian market dropped off corporate radar screens. But strong growth, high profits, enormous potential and massive improvements in the political and business environments are forcing senior management to take another look. Foreign investment is still low but increasing; annual flows are expected to triple over the next few years. (See Chapter 17 for a more detailed look at Russia and other CIS markets.)

Ukraine

After years of disappointing growth, a number of companies are reporting stronger growth in Ukraine than in Russia. The improvement in sales is reflected in the growing number of consumer goods companies that are considering upgrading their local presence to legal entity status and assessing how to better manage their Ukraine operations.

The rest of the CIS

As a general benchmark the "85-10-5" rule applies to doing business in the former Soviet Union for the majority of companies. This means that in most business sectors 85% of a company's business is carried out in Russia, 10% in Ukraine and 5% in the other republics. This of course excludes energy and commodity companies.

The Middle East

Business in the Middle East can be highly profitable, but for most companies it is subdued and below its potential as a result of complex geopolitics and restrictive local regimes. The Iraq war shuffled the geopolitical cards but big questions remain about the impact it will have on geopolitical stability and on economies and business. In any case, development in the region is unlikely to be substantial so long as the conflict between Israel and Palestinians continues.

Arab countries also underperform economically because many have relied on oil revenues and failed to develop human capital and other sectors. The *Arab Human Development Report 2002*, published by the UN Development Programme, shows the Arab world falling behind. Shrinking budget surpluses mean that social protection and soft jobs for the local population are becoming scarcer. Some 20% of Arabs live on less than $2 a day, and over the past 20 years annual income per head has grown at a mere 0.5%, slower than anywhere else in the world except sub-Saharan Africa.

Political failings and economic decline in the face of fast-growing populations raise fears about the stability of some countries in the Middle East. This in turn encourages talented people to look for opportunities for education and work elsewhere, while religious fundamentalists dissatisfied with their leadership adopt a more extremist line. All these factors have to be taken into account by businesses with a presence or seeking to establish a presence in the region.

Day-to-day operations are difficult in many Middle Eastern markets because of safety and security issues, red tape, inefficiency and corruption. Given the small volumes and the risks and obstacles to long-term market growth, it is hard (outside the energy, commodities, IT and services sectors) persuading management that it is worth the effort.

There is a big difference in sales trends among sectors: energy and commodity-related sales are doing well, as is the IT sector. But growth is much slower for most consumer goods companies and general manufacturers, which do not benefit from government tenders and partnerships in the energy sector.

Most companies outside the energy, commodities, IT and services sectors report steady to good business in Kuwait, Bahrain and Qatar, with annual growth trends of 15–20%, but few are excited by these markets because they are small. One of the stars of the region is the United Arab Emirates, especially Dubai.

Turkey

Turkey is an important emerging market in global terms, probably ranking sixth after China, Russia, India, Brazil and Iran. It has been one of the worst boom and bust markets for western companies since 1985, with financial, banking and political crises creating huge problems and uncertainties for western companies every few years. However, a new broom has appeared in Turkish politics in the form of the Justice and Development party (AKP), which came to power in 2002. After 13 years of chronic mismanagement under ten coalition governments, the elections resulted in a two-party parliament for the first time in 50 years and a single-party government for the first time in 15 years. The AKP, which has Islamist origins, is generally described in the western media as a "moderate, centre-right party". The government includes former ministers from the conservative Motherland Party. Recep Erdogan, the prime minister, is following a middle path and Abdullah Gul, the foreign minister, represents the party's moderate wing.

If Turkey can manage its debt repayment and related fiscal issues successfully, it has a chance to be a boom market in the second half of the 2000s. And if it were accepted for EU membership, an upswing would have much more chance of being sustainable than it has in the past. But will Turkey dig itself out of its debt hole without another major crisis? The risk of it not doing so is probably no more than 20%.

During the most recent crisis, western companies suffered falls in sales of 20–35% and margins were hit as companies cut prices. Although 2002 was a year of strong recovery, not all companies benefited equally. Sales of raw materials, semi-finished products and machinery did well and the outlook for the next few years is good. Consumer goods companies fared less well as consumers sought ever-cheaper products. However, the profits of western companies survived reasonably well as they exercised good overall cost control. Competition will remain fierce and some western companies will look to local production to build scale and brands and to benefit from cheaper local sourcing. But whatever the conditions, the daily operating environment remains tough, with red tape absorbing as much as 20% of management time, compared with only 4% in central and eastern Europe, according to a 1999 World Bank report.

What do western executives expect in the future? The 2001 crisis encouraged more scepticism and cynicism about the Turkish market, but the current potential for political and economic stability greatly improves Turkey's business prospects. In the past, when times have been good they have been very good indeed, and some sectors, such as electronic durables, can be extremely profitable. The trick is to manage your exposure. As one American consumer goods manager noted, echoing the consensus view of those operating in Turkey:

> *The number one issue is managing your receivables. This is more important than pricing or competition or anything else.*

Another manager from an office equipment company endorses this view:

> *We always make sure that we are prepared 100% for the next crisis so that whenever it happens we lose at most $50,000 and not $50m.*

In the end 2003 was a good year for the Turkish economy: real interest rates fell from 45% to below 10%, inflation fell from 29% to 18%; and western companies saw a noticeable improvement in sales. Turkey's relations with the IMF also improved, and by the end of the year relations with the United States were back on track after hiccups over Iraq. If the Cyprus issue is resolved in 2004, as some think it will be, in December 2004 the European Union may well give Turkey a date for EU entry some time in 2010–14.

Israel
It is not long since Israel was a thriving regional market and an engine

for growth for several neighbouring markets. Western companies were seeking to upgrade their operations from acting as distributors to setting up subsidiaries. Egypt, Lebanon, Jordan and Syria all benefited. But the prospects for western companies have turned sour. GDP growth has collapsed, the shekel has fallen, and inflation, unemployment and debt have all risen. Foreign investment has fallen by 65% since 2000, because of the Israeli–Palestinian conflict and the global decline in the IT industry, where Israel was strong. The conflict is costing the country $2 billion a year, hence the request for more aid from the United States. Israel is already the largest recipient of American aid (averaging $2 billion a year in the 1990s).

Retail sales have fallen dramatically as a result of unemployment and the fear of suicide bombers. Tighter government spending will also have a negative impact on growth. The outlook for business will remain bleak until some political progress is made.

Dubai
Dubai is the second biggest of seven emirates that form the United Arab Emirates (UAE). Abu Dhabi's ruling family dominates the federal UAE government and Dubai's non-sovereign status could cause problems regarding long-term legal security.

Sheikh Mohammed Bin Rashid Al Maktoum, the Crown Prince and effective ruler of Dubai, has focused on key sectors such as tourism, construction, media, financial services, retail and trade. New sectors for development include health care. Dubai's development of free zones has helped make it a regional centre and the relaxation of rules on property ownership have given the economy a huge boost.

It is believed by some that about one-third of western sales in Dubai end up in Iran. Large deals related to the delivery of gas from Qatar have ensured continued business interest in the energy sector.

Dubai has taken some steps towards market liberalisation, and the perception of political risk is lower than in some other Gulf states. Several companies located in Dubai report that there has been hardly any slowdown in business and no perceptible rise in tension despite what has been happening in other parts of the region. Dubai is a regional economic power house and an oasis of tranquillity – for the time being.

Saudi Arabia
Changed and changing relations with the United States will have a big effect on Saudi Arabia and a significant effect on the Middle East. The

relationship is more ambivalent than in the past but still close. The military pull-out of American forces in 2003 is a reversion to the position that existed before the 1991 war against Iraq following its invasion of Kuwait. The Saudi political system is under pressure to change, but any external attempt to institute western-style democracy would be likely to result in a fundamentalist government. Most of the people of Saudi Arabia have little time for the West and are becoming increasingly alienated from the Saudi regime as it is not providing enough jobs and not maintaining high levels of social security. King Fahd and his successor, Crown Prince Abdullah, are both over 80 years old and succession is likely to prove destabilising.

The economy is over-dependent on oil- and gas-related industries: oil export revenues were $60 billion in 2002 but will fall if, as is widely believed, the oil price drops. Saudi Arabia has a window of opportunity of about two years to put reforms in place and to stimulate the non-energy economy, but increasing political tensions will make successful reform hard to achieve. The budget surplus in 2000 was the first since 1982. In 2000–03 the population was growing 2% faster than annual GDP growth. GDP per head in oil-rich 1981 was $22,000, but it had slumped to $11,200 by 2003 and is expected to rise to only $12,000 by 2008. To generate enough jobs for all those entering the job market, the economy needs to grow at 6% per annum: in 1998–2003 average annual growth was less than 2% and in 2004–09 it is likely to be 3%.

But for all its risks and frustrations, the Saudi market has been holding up. Energy, IT and services companies report good sales. Even American consumer goods firms have been seeing sales growth of 10–20%, despite popular boycotts on some American brands. The problem is that volumes remain low for the size of the market. Companies also find the operational environment difficult and frustrating. Laws come and go, and business comes down to connections and families. One manager in the consumer goods sector was asked by his successful and entrepreneurial Saudi distributor: "Why don't you do more in Saudi and invest on the ground as you do elsewhere in the region?" The reply was "Frankly, the Saudi authorities don't want us here", meaning that western companies generally are not made welcome and business with western companies is seen as an annoyance rather than a means for economic co-operation and development.

Even if Saudi attitudes were to change, most companies would think hard before investing. An experienced veteran of emerging markets reflects the feeling of many in the western business community:

You don't need much risk analysis to know this place could blow anytime. Even before Iraq and the bombings in Saudi, anyone with any sense must know this is getting serious.

Iran

Iran has for several years been the market that most excites regional managers because of its potential. It is big, relatively wealthy, young and eager for western brands. Politics have largely frozen out American companies, while European companies have been allowed a relatively free hand to develop small but growing businesses.

Hopes of reconciliation with the United States have faded since September 11th 2001, despite Iran's long-term opposition to the Taliban, al-Qaeda and Saddam Hussein. The inclusion of Iran in President Bush's "axis of evil" has done business no favours for now. Political liberalisation has also suffered. The struggle between reformers under Mohammad Khatami, the president, and conservatives backed usually by Ayatollah Khamenei is likely to be long and drawn out.

American companies will continue to monitor the market. American government sanctions prevent direct sales by American firms, but American brand names are certainly visible, sold into Iran it is widely believed via Dubai. European corporations are making a killing in the market, and in consumer goods, food and beverages and equipment they have been reporting annual sales growth of 20–40%. European companies are taking advantage of the absence of American companies and setting up consumer goods manufacturing operations. Unilever (food and household products), Reemtsma (tobacco) and BAT (tobacco) appear likely to set up joint ventures and make acquisitions in Iran. They would follow Henkel, which acquired a majority stake in a detergent plant in 2002, and Cussons and Reckitt-Benckiser, which already produce locally. More companies are making exploratory visits to Iran and coming away with good first impressions, particularly the level of skills in the country and the openness of the people to doing business.

However, doing business in Iran today could be compared with doing business in the former Soviet Union in about 1988. The people may be keen, but there is much centralisation and unwieldy bureaucracy.

Iraq

There are many imponderables in assessing what the future holds for

Iraq and what its potential is for western companies. Rebuilding the Iraqi energy infrastructure will be a priority, but it will take two or three years before Iraqi oil output is back to 75–90% of full capacity.

Africa

Africa is largely a human tragedy and a commercial mess. It is the weakest emerging market region in terms of attracting business, and it has slipped backwards while the rest of the world has moved on. In the 1990s real GDP per head in the continent actually fell and, on average, is lower than it was in the 1960s. Africa's share of world GDP is now 1%, a decrease of one-third over the past 50 years; its share of world exports has decreased by two-thirds over the same period. In 1980 Africa accounted for 28% of global foreign investment; 20 years later the figure was only 7%.

Too much African infrastructure is designed to ship out exports and not enough is built for internal trade and markets. Many economies are dependent on volatile commodity prices. Intra-regional trade, although rising, still accounts for only 10% of African exports. IMF programmes have done little for Africa: either the funds were misdirected in the first place or they have been squandered or stolen by local officials. Debt is a huge burden, and many African countries still spend more of their annual budgets on interest payments to the West than on education or health.

Africa needs a concerted combination of aid, trade and implementation of the debt relief agreements already signed. This might encourage reform and support programmes such as the New Economic Partnership for Africa's Development (NEPAD), which promises good governance and a better business environment. But Africa's economic and political track record does not inspire confidence, let alone hope. Development of the oil industry in Nigeria, and especially in western Africa, will mean that revenues of some $200 billion will flow into African government treasuries in the next ten years. But how much of the money will be put to good use, and how much will be wasted on prestige projects or diverted into private bank accounts?

Africa is also blighted by AIDS. UN reports estimate that in 2002 sub-Saharan Africa accounted for 71% of the more than 40m adults and children living with AIDS around the world, and that average sub-Saharan life expectancy was 47 years in 2002, 15 years lower than it would have been without AIDS. Human development in the region will be harmed more in the coming years as more children become orphans and do not attend school. On the economic front, countries will suffer from more labour and skill shortages, especially as men in the age range 20–45 fall victim to AIDS. Medical costs, both public and private, will increase; a few companies are beginning to provide specific medical and insurance coverage but this is unlikely to become prevalent.

GDP will grow more slowly and poverty levels will rise, which will have long-term effects over the next decade and beyond. It is estimated that in 2012 the South African economy will be 20% smaller than it would have been without AIDS. In a survey of South African managers, 60% thought the epidemic was a "serious threat" at the national level but only 20% thought it would seriously harm their business. This may prove to be an optimistic assessment. Outsiders are taking a gloomier view. Investors are now asking for premium rates of return of 18–20% in South Africa and 25–30% in the rest of sub-Saharan Africa on account of the higher risk associated with AIDS, according to the Economist Intelligence Unit and Business Map.

It is therefore not surprising that the African continent is overall a poor market. The exceptions are energy and mining companies, which do well in several countries. Sales for western consumer goods and pharmaceuticals companies will, on average, grow slowly if at all over the next few years. However, the big IT companies are reporting reasonable business, especially in South Africa but also in West Africa and parts of North Africa. Some mobile telecoms and food and beverages companies are also doing well.

Consumer goods companies are reporting good growth in some parts of the continent, especially when they enter new markets in francophone West Africa. Western commercial interest in eastern Africa picked up in 2002–03, but this was not sustained as the markets did not meet expectations. However, companies will continue to monitor Kenya, Uganda and Tanzania in the coming years for any improvements in this potentially interesting subregion. Even Nigeria (the world's most corrupt place to do business, according to Transparency International – and there is a lot of competition for the top spot) has proved to be a profitable market for companies that have been able to build onshore operations to circumvent tariff barriers.

For most manufacturing and consumer goods companies, the continent boils down to a triangle of three key markets: Egypt, Morocco and South Africa. For most of the period 2000–03 these markets struggled or were volatile.

Egypt

For most western companies, the Egyptian market was at a ten-year low in 2003. The retail market is small for the size of population: it was $15 billion in 2003 and is expected to rise to only $17 billion by 2007. The experience of Sainsbury, a UK supermarket chain, which abandoned the market in 2001 after two disastrous years, made many investors cautious. However, Carrefour, a French firm, is entering the market via a partnership and hopes to build four hypermarkets. Some telecoms investors are experiencing 20–25% growth but in a more competitive market. Western investment banks have concerns about Egyptian banking policy. Some western IT companies complain that business is severely hampered by a lack of dollars and liquidity. A further obstacle is the lack of tax deductions and exemptions, and even in free-trade zones the logistics can be difficult. According to a manager of a European chemicals company in 2003:

> Getting into the Egyptian market with our industrial or
> consumer products is so tough. Saudi and Jordan are currently
> much better markets for us.

It can be argued that the results of the past 10–20 years indicate that Egypt's economic liberalisation reform policies have gone the way of those of Latin America. The elimination of the currency peg in January 2003 was a step in the right direction. Unfortunately, it failed because the government did not dispose of enough currency to support a significantly lower exchange rate and because the timing was extremely difficult against the backdrop of the invasion of Iraq.

The Egyptian market is tough for most companies. Even where sales growth is good, profit levels are relatively disappointing and profit repatriation is a huge headache. Some companies in the consumer goods sector are considering manufacturing locally as a way of handling foreign-exchange shortages and customs problems, but political and commercial risks make it a difficult decision. Indeed, the problems are such that it is diffucult for regional managers to present a convincing case to headquarters for making Egypt part of the corporate strategy.

Morocco

Morocco is about the tenth largest market in the Middle East and Africa (referred to as the MEA region). Following the inauguration of King Mohammed VI hopes of reform rose, but the influence of domestic vested interests (large business families, the army and the interior ministry) made sure that these did not develop. The business community sees the king as being unwilling to reform or incapable of taking on the opposition to it and driving the process through. But efforts to open up the market will continue. Tourism is the top foreign-currency earner, but the industry was damaged by the September 11th terrorist attacks in the United States and the 2003 terrorist attack in Casablanca. Morocco is an associate EU member, which helps FDI flows and attracts investment into telecoms, cement, the food industry and components manufacturing. It is also moving towards a free-trade agreement with the United States. But investors complain of a non-transparent investment environment, an out-dated labour code, a poor judicial service and excessive red tape.

South Africa

The South African economy is the most important on the continent. Many western companies doing business there in recent years have experienced tough and volatile times. But enough companies have done well enough to keep the market on the corporate radar screen. Monetary and fiscal management by the government and the Reserve Bank is by far the best in the region and compares well with financial management anywhere in the world. However, as in most emerging markets the authorities are faced with the challenges of managing growth and the need for lower inflation. Furthermore, the rand is a volatile currency as a result of dependency on commodity exports, the gold price and the quoting of the stocks of many large South African companies on foreign exchanges (some 60% of trading in the rand is conducted offshore). The big threat to South Africa's longer-term future – and the big question for the South African economy – is whether it can overcome the scepticism of foreign direct investors and the financial markets and persuade them to provide enough funding to support economic development and the currency.

As in other parts of sub-Saharan Africa, poverty is widespread. Income differentials are high, 35–40% of the black population is unemployed and some 45% of the population live in poverty. Some 1m skilled whites have left the country and only 6% of the population have university degrees, mostly whites. The government is attempting to address the imbalance with black empowerment laws, requiring companies to train black managers and develop black-owned firms by transferring equity stakes and favouring them in procurement. It is a brave attempt to keep South Africa from going the way of neighbouring Zimbabwe, but few multinationals are willing to take the risk of participating in the experiment when there are other locations begging for investment. Other factors deterring investment include: AIDS, increasing trade-union power and violent crime.

Asia

China

China has emerged as the dominant regional player. Since it joined the World Trade Organisation (WTO), the market has been opening with considerable benefits for western companies. China's exports rose from 2% of the world total in 1993 to 5% in 2002; they are expected to grow in 2004–06, boosting GDP growth by an additional 1% a year until 2012. FDI flows, already the world's highest at over $50 billion per year, are expected to double by 2008. The surge in the Chinese economy has been phenomenal: average growth of 8.5% since 1980 is the largest sustained growth recorded in economic history. China is increasingly important globally: in 2002 it accounted for some 60% of the world's import and export growth. It is also fast becoming the "workshop of the world": in 2002 it consumed some 21% of the world's traded alumina, 24% of its zinc and 17% of its copper, according to Deutsche Bank and the *Financial Times*. Much of Latin America's GDP growth in 2002–03 was attributable to surging raw material exports to China, and the country surpassed the United States in 2002 as the world's major destination for foreign direct investment, attracting $53 billion.

China may be sucking in huge amounts of investment (as Mexican competitors, among others, complain) because of its low wage structure. However, for regions competing with China, such as central Europe, there are some persuasive arguments in favour of making investments in them rather than in China:

- higher productivity;
- better just-in-time delivery;
- cheaper distribution costs with regard to European and American markets (transportation costs have been underestimated by several companies investing in China);
- lower duties in the EU and NAFTA;
- the attraction, for American and European managers, of working in markets that are culturally closer to their own (some western managers complain of the difficulty of building personal relationships with their Chinese partners, for example).

China's economy was and still is dependent on government pump-priming. The new leadership will face tremendous challenges in restructuring and closing down thousands of state enterprises and laying off millions of workers when the global economy is giving less support to Chinese exports. Structural reforms will soon have to replace pump-priming.

The political risks in China are high, as pressure for democratisation must increase. One of the effects of joining the WTO will be to increase unemployment by 50m–100m, because increased competition from imports will bankrupt parts of heavy industry and undermine the weak agricultural sector, leading to more job losses. Out of a population of 1.3 billion, 180m are already estimated to be unemployed in the towns and countryside, with another 200m underemployed in rural areas. Economic dangers include high levels of non-performing loans in the banking sector, weak mechanisms for pricing capital (such as underdeveloped stockmarkets and currency transfer restrictions), overinvestment, oversupply of products, and too few independent institutions and courts to monitor economic activity. Liberalisation in the banking sector and of capital flows, or excessive revaluation of the currency, could result in the worst emerging-market crash in history and would have a severe impact on the global economy, not least because China holds more than $100 billion in American assets and would want to repatriate a substantial amount of those dollars in the event of a crisis.

South-East Asia

The Asian tigers have found it difficult to regain their reputation since the 1997–98 crisis. On some criteria, South-East Asia is better off now than it was immediately after the crisis. All countries except Indonesia have better positions overall in short-term debt and overall debt levels. Current accounts and budget deficits are under control, apart from in Taiwan, Indonesia and Malaysia. But much of this better position stems from the devaluation in 1997–98. The nagging question is: did the ASEAN (Association of South-East Asian Nations, comprising Brunei, Cambodia, Indonesia, Laos, Malaysia, Myanmar, Philippines, Singapore, Thailand and Vietnam) countries do enough after the last crisis in terms of cleaning up their banking sector and restructuring their economies, or did they rely too much on the easy benefits of exchange rates? Many think they took the easy option.

The ASEAN markets are still suffering from a weak American market, in particular the IT market. Singapore, Malaysia and Taiwan posted neg-

Compared with China, other markets in the region are losing out and will have to adapt to the new giant. In a poll conducted in Asia in 2002, multinationals were asked what proportion of their corporate focus (time and investment) would be dedicated to certain regional markets in 2006 compared with 2002. The main results are shown in Table 16.3.

Table 16.3 **Proportion of corporate focus dedicated to regional markets (%)**

	2002	2006
China	22	33
Hong Kong	17	10
Japan	12	10
South Korea	8	8
Singapore	12	7
India	35	6

Source: The Economist Corporate Network, Asia

Nevertheless, western companies have not had an easy time in China. Corporate order books, which are the best way to assess the market as official Chinese growth figures can be unreliable, show a mixed picture. Profitability has apparently been low for many companies operating in China (although there was a lot of transfer pricing which lessened the tax burden so it is difficult to assess real profitability). But after a decade of relatively unspectacular results, entry into the WTO and other changes in the operating environment transformed the market's potential.

For many western companies, China will again be in favour for the next few years, and increasing investment in the country will mean less for all other regions. Emerging markets that rely mainly on low wage costs and labour-intensive industries have good reasons to be frightened of the expanding China.

Will it go wrong?

China's venture into the global economy could bring with it the usual problems faced by emerging markets. The economy has been protected over the last 20 years because the country has kept out of the globalisation process and retained currency controls. As the WTO process unfolds and the economy opens up, financial stability will come under increasing pressure. There are those who say that China is due for an emerging-market blow-up, as in Asia in 1997 and Russia in 1998.

ative growth in 2001, which is not surprising given that they and Hong Kong and Philippines depend on the American market for 25% of their GDP and some 40–50% of their exports. But they were able to pick up and enjoyed growth of 2–4% in 2002, largely through increasing trade flows among themselves and directing more efforts to the Chinese market. Domestic demand also took up some of the slack. The ASEAN economies are predicted to post growth of 3–5% in 2004–06, but the outlook for growth is more volatile in Singapore and Taiwan because of their greater dependency on the global electronics industry.

The fall in the value of the US dollar will probably require governments in the region to start competing on exchange rates and to adopt measures to lower the value of their own currencies, or at least to limit appreciation against the dollar. Intensified Chinese competition in regional and global markets will exacerbate the region's problems.

Western corporate strategies: China and ASEAN

It is hard for the smaller Asian markets to prove their relevance as China blossoms. Total FDI into Asia has been declining. China, meanwhile, attracts 80% of FDI coming into Asia and flows are increasing. It is likely to get $60–75 billion a year in 2004–06. Internal trade barriers prevent the ASEAN region turning itself into an open market of 500m people; instead it consists of small, tricky markets. It is not a fully functioning free-trade area, and not all markets or all major products are involved, so there is no consistency for western investors. If these flaws were removed, this would greatly benefit consumer goods, electronics and auto companies. Lower tariffs have already helped some companies.

ASEAN markets are becoming less reliant on the American economy and exporting more to China, which imports more from the rest of Asia than does Japan. These smaller markets will have to focus on their specialisations and relative advantages in their relations with China. This will mean going up the production value chain and following Singapore, South Korea and Taiwan, or going for niche markets in energy and foodstuffs. ASEAN countries will lose some manufacturing to China, but they can increase supplies and services to their massive neighbour. China is currently a large net exporter of light labour-intensive manufactures and a large net importer of machinery, equipment and primary materials. It will also seek to invest its large capital surplus abroad, which will benefit the region.

Western companies will want to reap the benefits of the huge Chinese market while not being too dependent on it for their regional strategy. Most companies want to retain operations in both China and the rest of ASEAN and build operational synergies. Philips, an electronics consumer goods manufacturer, for example, has moved manufacturing from Singapore to China and senior management to Hong Kong to be closer to the Chinese market, but the company retains a strong R&D presence in Singapore. Such a two-pronged approach seeks to establish production bases throughout the region with a focus on China, and to continue to consolidate operations in ASEAN so as to achieve benefits of scale from an eventual ASEAN free-trade zone and an eventual free-trade zone including China.

The pressure to rethink strategy with regard to Asia is also coming from headquarters. In late 1999, more as a response to pressures on corporate earnings rather than a reaction to the Asian crisis, many global headquarters took a new approach to the ASEAN region. They realised that they had been lax in their operating structures in the region and less demanding in judging earnings results and returns on investment. Regional managers were asked to increase top-line revenue and cut costs by downsizing and closing some local regional offices. They will be expected to continue this leaner and meaner approach over the coming years and will consequently re-examine supply chains, with more companies moving to China.

India

Of the three big markets to break into – China, Russia and India – India will almost certainly take the bronze medal for trading and investor interest over the next few years for various reasons.

In the first place, it is a difficult market. Multinationals complain of strong local competition, low purchasing power, a north-south divide, strong social and cultural resistance to western brands, and widespread corruption. Investors often allude to "the seven burdens" of doing business in India: the cost of power and utilities; the cost of borrowing; red tape; corruption; heavy sales and local taxes; expensive and slow transport; and inflexible labour markets.

Although the annual growth rate of exports has been around 10% in recent years, the economic mood has been gloomy since the late 1990s because of non-performing loans and poor corporate profitability. Non-performing loans stem from the huge fiscal deficit, which the government cannot shake off. As a result, the government does all the borrowing and crowds out private-sector borrowing and investment. Real interest rates are therefore too high. Half of government receipts are spent on the domestic debt burden, so few resources are left for infrastructure development. GDP growth seems a healthy 5–6%, but according to Manohan Sing, India's architect of reform and former finance minister, the country needs to be reporting annual growth of 7–8% in order to catch up, in terms of development, reduce poverty and outpace population growth. Within the growth structure, there is too much reliance on the services sector, including telecoms, banking, IT, and not enough on staple industries.

A succession of scandals, political infighting and tensions with Pakistan has distracted the government – which is hampered by being formed from a 23-party coalition. As the economy slows, it becomes more likely that the government will lose the political will to embark on such things as deregulation, reform of labour practices, privatisation of public utilities, reducing public-sector subsidies and reforming the capital markets.

On the plus side, India's IT enclaves are excellent, it attracts investment into outsourcing, shared services facilities and call centres, and it has excellent human resources to operate these investments. One human resources problem is emigration of clever people.

Latin America

It is a brave and rare person who can put hand on heart and say: "I believe that in the next few years the IMF's plans for Latin America will ensure stable GDP and commercial growth in the region." Would any western company bank on Argentina and Brazil overcoming their current difficulties, avoiding boom and bust developments and acting as a steady motor for sustainable growth in the region?

Nevertheless, Latin America is a comfort zone for many US companies, even though the economic and political outlook is considerably worse than, say, in central Europe or Russia. The reasons relate to history and US corporate experience and culture. It can be frustrating for managers operating in non-Latin American markets when companies' US headquarters want to stick only or predominantly with this region. But their faith in Latin America will not prevent the region from attracting less foreign investment than other emerging markets. Its share of emerging-market investment was 28% in 2003 compared with 36% in 2000, and it is likely to stagnate at about 25–27% up to 2010 as China, Russia and central Europe remain more attractive.

Both the protectionist, statist policies of the 1970s and 1980s and the free-trade, globalisation, open-markets model of the 1990s have failed

Latin America. The impact is clear. The World Health Organisation reckons that 20% of Argentinian children suffer from malnutrition in a country that has 50m cattle and 39m people and is the world's fourth largest food exporter. Since the beginning of 2002, 1m jobs have been lost, leaving half the population living in poverty and 20% destitute. As J.F. Kennedy once noted: "The real menace in Latin America is not communism, it is poverty and income inequality." Things have not changed much since Kennedy's day. Latin America still has the highest levels of income inequality in the world. The World Bank calculates that Latin American annual growth needs to average 4% for the next ten years in order to haul only 50% of the region's population out of extreme poverty by 2015.

The outlook is that the region will stumble along as Argentina slowly digs itself out of its crisis and regional trade picks up. Brazil's future hangs on a thread and the Lula government has a tricky balancing act to perform. Other economies in the region are struggling for different reasons.

Argentina

Nestor Kirchner, Argentina's president, is trying to make the best of it with an economic policy focusing on export-led growth supported by a flexible exchange-rate policy. He has stated that he does not want external debt repayments to force a compromise in the recovery programme. This is the crux of the matter. After a deep three-year recession, economic decline may have hit the bottom but the outlook for the next 2–3 years is extremely challenging. The flexible and lower exchange rate has benefited the Argentinian economy. Most western investors have put their businesses on hold, despite recording some bounce back from the depths of the recent crisis. Argentina's future remains uncertain, but in 2003 the government did negotiate forcefully with the IMF to obtain what most observers thought was a very generous debt rescheduling deal.

Brazil

The thumping election victory of Luiz Inacio Lula da Silva in October 2002 showed that the Brazilian people wanted social change that would involve more jobs and fairer income distribution. Lula's remarks on being elected helped stabilise the markets, although inflation did rise. He gave a commitment not to default on debt and to follow the broad outlines of the IMF programme agreed with his predecessor.

Brazil's problem is low growth and a high debt burden. GDP growth in 2002 was 1.7%; it crept back to 2% in 2003 but will remain at about 2.5% in 2004–06. This is too low a level to help Brazil resolve its debt crisis. The trap of the IMF funding proffered in 2002 is that the money will be released only if the government runs a primary surplus (the budget position before debt repayments are taken into account) of at least 3.75%. This does not look compatible with decent growth.

As with Argentina, the main hope lies with exports, which have benefited and will continue to benefit from a more competitive exchange rate. The weaker currency, government incentives and tariff protection within Mercosur have enticed many automotive investors, including Ford Motors, General Motors, DaimlerChrysler and Volkswagen, which continue to expand projects. Other sectors with potential include utilities and food processing. But as in India and other big emerging markets, investors face persistent problems. There is even a special term, the *custo Brazil*, which means the cost of business derived from high taxes, red tape, expensive financing, infrastructural deficiencies and relatively weak human resources.

Mexico

Mexico survived best in the region until 2000 but then caught the contagion from the US economy and has struggled with low growth since. Mexico is one of many markets facing the investment challenge from China as more US and European companies turn their attention to that market. When the US economy picks up, the North American Free Trade Agreement (NAFTA) will shine again. Samsung demonstrated its faith in Mexico when it opened its largest white-goods plant in Latin America there.

The economic fate of Mexico is largely dependent on US trade links since NAFTA was signed. Another factor in the country's economic health is the increasing attraction of China as a manufacturing base. The Mexican authorities are probably looking now just as much at trends in China as in the United States.

Venezuela

Venezuela's economy collapsed by 10% in 2001 and 13% in 2002 as a result of political turmoil. It bounced back in 2003, but sustainable growth is elusive.

Regional outlook

The main problem for Argentina, Brazil and Uruguay is how to grow their way out of recession and low growth. Without this, there may be a series of hand-to-mouth palliatives, and the region may face underlying macroeconomic weakness for the next five years with recurring cyclical crises.

Is Latin America really better off 20 years after the start of market liberalisation? The current state of affairs fails to provide long-term, credible, sustainable growth and development for the people of the region and for multinational companies that want to do business there.

17 Russia: a detailed look

Russia will be our biggest market in Europe in ten years.

Peter Brabeck, CEO of Nestlé, speaking in November 2002

We invested a couple of million in Russia a few years ago. It was the best business decision of my life.

Regional manager, American pharmaceuticals company

For the last two years, Russia has posted the best sales growth in the world.

Regional vice-president of one of the world's largest IT companies

China and Russia are our key growth markets in the world for the next five years.

Regional manager of one of the world's largest soft drinks companies

One of the major themes of this book is that many western multinationals are ignorant of opportunities in emerging markets and how to develop their business in those markets. The Russian market is a prime example of western prejudice and ignorance.

The experience of hundreds of western companies operating in this market would indicate that media portryal of Russia as a place where you will get cheated or even killed by the Russian mafia if you attempt to do business there is simplistic and wrong – and becoming more wrong. The level of success in the Russian market is one of the best-kept or misunderstood secrets in the business world, although no one would deny that the market is difficult, painful and problematic.

Where in the world?

Until mid-2002 it was difficult to get the attention and commitment of senior management to start to do something in Russia or to develop an existing business. There was an "endless internal debate on Russia". Today, however, an increasing number of companies are willing at least to look at Russia. More American and European CEOs and board members are visiting Moscow and starting to listen to the arguments.

Western CEOs are focusing more and more on top-line growth, and as they see other developed or some emerging markets flat or crumbling, they ask: how do we get sustainable sales growth, where do we get it and where will we get it for the next 5–10 years? For global multinationals such as Ford, among many others, the answer is often China, Russia and India, in that order. Russia is getting more attention, and no wonder, as firms report sales growth of 30–45%.

The reason Russia has been ignored in the boardrooms of major multinationals probably has a lot to do with the history and politics of the 20th century. Many board members grew up in a culture where, since 1945, Russia and the rest of the Soviet Union were the number one enemy and bogeyman. It still colours their thinking, as is clear from what the manager for Europe of one of the best-branded corporate names in the world said recently:

> We do some good but below potential business in Russia. But when I brought this on to the agenda our CEO screamed at me that "we will not do business with those damned communists".

What's good about doing business in Russia?
Growth in western sales is among the best in the world
Sales figures of 30–40% are strong by any criteria but few businesses anywhere can grow organically at that pace, and many have been trying to gauge what the "sustainability figure" is. The consensus among companies in all sectors is that they are aiming for about 20% annual growth over the next five years. This is not a small target, and 20% is not set in concrete. The point is the relativity. Companies that were achieving growth of 40–50% in 2001–02 feel that a sustainable figure during the period 2003–07 is around 20%, about half of what they were achieving in earlier years.

The example of a European food company reflects the reality. It boasted 40% top-line growth in 2000 and 50% in 2001. But recognising increasing competition, domestic brand challenges and a perceived slow-down in liquidity, and factoring in the oil-price risk, the company has adopted two scenarios for its five-year plan. The best case seeks annual top-line growth of 20% and the worst case settles for growth of 10%. Those formulating the plan are confident that they can achieve the best case but see no harm in presenting a worst-case scenario of 10% for budgetary reasons.

Table 17.1 **Western sales growth in selected commercial sectors, 2001–06 (%)**

	2001	2002	2003	2004	2005	2006
Pharmaceuticals	50–60	35	15	23	18	15
Over-the-counter pharmaceuticals	125	40	25	25	20	16
Chemicals & industrials	35	35	33	28	25	20
Fast-moving consumer goods	40–50	40	35	30	25	22
Food & beverages	26	25	25	20	18	18
Information technology	25–35	33	35	30	28	25

Source: Daniel Thorniley

The figures in Table 17.1 refer to average organic sales growth based on private surveys carried out by the authors of some 100 western companies. Some companies will have reported significantly higher results after large new investments or significant jumps in headcount; there will also be wide variations. As one IT company noted in mid 2003:

> *Depending on whether we win one or two large tenders in 2003–04, our sales can rise 150% and we are quietly hopeful.*

Pharmaceuticals sales have fallen more quickly than sales in other sectors for industry-specific reasons: certification, registration and VAT.

Most western executives believe they can build a sustainable business
Russia appears to be set for a fairly long period of normality. Looking back over the past decade, economic and business development for western companies was good compared with other emerging markets in Latin America or those such as Turkey. Business grew well from 1990 to the first dip in 1993 and then surged for several years before the rouble crash of 1998. The bounce-back was reasonably quick for most companies, and they are again reporting solid results and higher sales than just before the 1998 crisis.

One manager of a western health company summed up the situation in 2002, saying: "The real work starts now." He meant that in the 1990s there were surges, volatility and the 1998 crash. The trend thereafter would be for some steady slog, steady growth models and managing corporate expectations – most of the normal issues of day-to-day business anywhere in the world. For those who enjoy working in Russia, this should not mean that doing business there will be as exciting as doing business in, say, Luxembourg. The Russian business environment may be becoming more normal, but there will be highs and lows, surprises and laughs on the way.

For many western companies the Russian market is highly profitable
Average profit margins in 2001–03 ranged from 15% to 20%. Some companies had focused on growth in market share rather than profit margin. A manager working for a European pharmaceuticals company noted in 2003: "We have had great growth recently but now my aim is to get the profits up." Large consumer goods companies often report profit levels three times higher than in western Europe and 50–80% higher than in central Europe. For many consumer goods, food and beverages, packaging, chemicals and machinery companies, Russia is their most profitable market. According to a manager of a big international consumer goods company:

> We aim for and achieve profit margins of 8–12% in the West,
> 12–15% in central and eastern Europe and 17–21% in Russia.

Tetra Pak, a packaging company, notes that Russia is its second most profitable market in the world after Brazil.

Why is the market profitable? Several companies have found that they can still charge premium prices for products in Russia, whereas this is no longer the case in larger eastern European markets such as Poland, Hungary and the Czech Republic (although pricing pressure is increasing in Russia). Many Russian customers – both individuals and businesses – are willing to pay premium prices for quality products. They are not stupid and will rarely be taken in by glib marketing: if a product can differentiate itself on quality, there is a better chance in this market that the customer will pay more. This has been a trend since soon after the collapse of the rouble in 1998 and was underlined in a telling way by the regional manager of a western food company:

> The Russians really do look for quality – obviously those who
> have discretionary purchasing power. They want quality and
> will pay for it. In the food sector especially, they won't buy the
> rubbish that the average German consumer will eat.

This may have implications as the retail sector takes off in Russia. Going for the discount market may not – at least initially – be the key to success for retailers as they engage in price wars. Nevertheless, the pressure of market forces will surely drive the market downwards eventually, if with a little more resistance than in other markets. In the short to medium term, western consumer goods, food and beverages companies in Russia can tell western retailers that "you don't have to impose your global strategies and price structures here because it's a different and more discerning market". And they may be right.

Moscow is cool

The managing director of one of the world's largest consumer goods companies said recently: "Moscow is a cool place." She was not referring to the climate but to the atmosphere of excitement and of things happening. This comment has serious and positive implications for human resources issues. In the past a posting to Russia was not always regarded as a career-enhancing move or an enjoyable prospect, but this has now changed. The manager mentioned above says she is "bombarded with requests from colleagues to come and work for me in Russia". One German bank reckons that in 2003 there were some 30,000 western expatriates whose term in Moscow was scheduled to end and who did not want to leave. Now that business is booming and is easier to conduct, western executives are keen to go there. This is also important when seen against a background in which salaries for Russian staff are rising and some companies are considering increasing the number of expatriate workers.

Growth prospects in the regions

The Russian regions can be good ammunition for country and regional managers in corporate debates because they can be used as a positive factor in the drive for organic geographical growth as well as a stabilising factor in managing corporate expectations.

The Russian Federation is broken down into 89 administrative units or regions. In 2001–03 most western consumer goods and food and beverage companies were doing business in 5–10 such regions. The main ones for business are Moscow city, Moscow region, St Petersburg and the Leningrad region (curiously, when the city changed its name, the surrounding region did not). Only a handful of western companies do business in more than 20–30 regions, including Dandy Stimorol, a Danish chewing gum company bought by Cadbury Schweppes in 2002, Coca-Cola and Pepsico.

As competition tightens in Moscow and St Petersburg and their surrounding regions, more western companies are looking at the relatively untouched markets of the outer regions. There are a number of "usual suspects" of second-rank regions, including Yekaterinburg, Nizhnii Novgorod, Samara, Rostov, Novisibirsk and Novgorod. They offer good scope for organic business growth, but they are no panacea for business development as a large number (as many as 40–50) are not really interesting for western companies because their populations are too small and/or too poor or the regions are geographically too remote. However, overall, the regions offer business opportunities that do not exist to the same extent in central Europe. A good comparison is China, where western companies are expanding out of Beijing and the coastal zones into the interior regions.

Managers can use the regions like a concertina in their budgeting process, expanding or contracting at their own discretion the number of regions into which they plan to expand business in order to meet budget targets set by headquarters. A manager in Moscow may consider expanding into five new regions in the next budget year, but if a tough budget is set, the expansion can be ratcheted up to seven or eight new regions. However, if by good fortune a growth target is set which can be met with some ease, the manager may choose to go for only two or three new regions instead of five.

Competition in Russia is not yet fierce

Competition is not as intense as it is in some of the central and eastern European markets. It is reasonable to say that in terms of competition, Russia is 3–4 years behind Poland and 1–3 years behind Hungary and the Czech Republic. However, it is catching up quickly. The type of competition is also different from the core central and eastern European markets, as a manager of a consumer goods company noted:

> We bump into each other in the market but we are not yet at the stage of savaging each other for 1% of market share, not even in Moscow. The market is big enough and the regions will give a lot of scope for geographical growth. But the cake will stop expanding in size and then market share will become the driver.

How long will the window of opportunity for other competitors to enter the market stay open? For those not in the market, this comment from the managing director of a major western company will be food for thought: "We think anyone who wants to be a player must be in during 2003–04." A Danish executive noted the change in the competitive environment:

> *In the mid-1990s we were making a lot of money in Russia for not doing very much. Now we're making a lot of money in Russia, but we are working damned hard for it.*

The retail sector is improving

The form of competition for consumer goods companies will change radically as western retailers flood into the Russian market. Western retailers will also introduce and enforce their global business models, which will squeeze the margins of consumer goods companies. This trend is already apparent in central and eastern Europe.

In 2002 some 500,000 square metres of quality retail space opened in Moscow, where retailers are attracted by the growth in incomes and retail sales. Moscow has a population of at least 8m with an income per head of almost $6,000 (almost five times higher than St Petersburg). Muscovites spend 45% of their income on food and alcohol, 20% on other non-food consumer products, 16% on shoes and clothing, 5% on electronics, 3% on public transport and just 4% on housing and 1% on education. The proportion of retail spending is significantly higher than in other European cities. Currently, just one-third of retail spending is in "normal" shops and supermarkets; outdoor markets and kiosks account for the remaining two-thirds.

Players such as Metro, a wholesaler, Spar and AVA, both retailers, have monitored the success of IKEA, a Swedish home furnishings chain, which is planning its third store in Russia. After just two years in business, the first IKEA store in Moscow accounts for 11% of IKEA's global sales. The plan is to increase this to 30% by 2007, with sales rising from $60m in 2002 to $1 billion in 2007.

Political risk is manageable

In a 2002 survey of 200 western executives who are part of The Economist Corporate Network east European peer group, 98% of respondents said that political risk was getting better, 2% said it was stable and no one said it was getting worse.

The stability that Vladimir Putin, Russia's president, has generated has been good for business. Russians in general appreciate having more stability and this is helping to make the population feel that they have a stake in the future. It is also generating confidence among Russian entrepreneurs as they do business with western partners and start to buy up companies in the West.

However, Russia is still a country in transition and its institutions are weak, so the following risks need to be considered.

- Politics could become volatile because Putin does not have a natural political constituency; his power base is merely the "party of power".
- "Russia has lost an empire and is still looking for a role" – and so Putin may face more administrative opposition from the military and their supporters if the current "love fest" with the United States results in few tangible benefits.
- Living standards for many are still poor, especially in the rural and more remote regions; but a backlash is unlikely because there is no political organisation through which this dissatisfaction can be expressed.
- Any significant fall in the oil price would put pressure on the budget, government spending and consumption in the cities, which could pose a political threat of upheaval.
- More active and organised opposition may develop as some powerful economic and political interests are affected by the reorganisation that has started to take place in the energy sector, utilities and the railways.
- A major failing of the political system, the lack of modernisation of Russia's institutional bodies and its civil service, could give rise to problems.

Nevertheless, the political risk appears to be manageable and the political outlook stable for the next few years at least.

Economic challenges

For most of 2001–03, consumer demand and energy exports drove growth. But local industry fared less well and western companies reported difficult business. Russia is still too dependent on the energy sector, and more needs to be done to drive domestic investment into non-energy sectors and to develop small and medium-sized businesses. Domestic investment fell by 70% in the 1990s. A revival began in 1999–2001, but the trend slowed in 2002 when investment in the non-energy sector slumped, partly because of temporary changes in the tax law on investments. Domestic investment rebounded strongly by 12% in 2002, and growth of 5-7% in 2004-08 is predicted. But Russia will not reach its potential for growth until structural reforms are complete in the utilities and railway sectors – a huge undertaking with no guarantee of success.

It will take up to ten years to clean up the banking sector and get it in shape. Russian banks provide only 6% of the finance required by Russian enterprises, which obtain the remainder predominantly from re-invested profits, returning flight capital or western partnerships. Western banks are not very interested in investing in the market, although Citibank has dipped into the local retail market, where the lead has been taken by Austrian banks.

The outlook for inflation and the rouble is reassuring

After the 1998 crisis, the government focused on boosting growth and competitiveness and buttressing foreign-currency reserves. The consequent decrease in the value of the rouble meant that inflation would not come down quickly. But as the December 2003 Duma elections approached, to be followed by presidential elections in March 2004, the government wanted to curb inflation more quickly and was therefore willing to allow the rouble to strengthen. As it happened, high oil prices in 2002-03 and the weaker dollar ensured a strong rouble for most of 2002 and 2003. Real appreciation of the rouble against the dollar was 5-8% in 2002 and 15% in 2003.

Despite the currency appreciation, inflation is unlikely to fall rapidly because of:

- increases in wages and pensions;
- fairly robust consumer demand;
- liberalisation of housing and utility prices;
- the growth of money in circulation as a result of the underdeveloped domestic debt market.

Budget surpluses, falling inflation and a strong oil price will ensure that the rouble remains strong. Could there be any dangers in this? After several years of steady appreciation, the rouble has now recouped some 90% of its real value before the 1998 crash. Some say that because the rouble was then heavily overvalued, a severe adjustment should be anticipated. Those who take a different view point to the fact Russia is no longer sticking to a misguided currency peg to the dollar or financing

Table 17.2 **Key economic indicators, 2000–07 (%)**

	2000	2001	2002	2003	2004	2005	2006	2007
GDP	8.8	5.0	4.4	6.2	5.0	4.7	4.4	4.6
Inflation year-end	20.2	18.6	15.1	13.1	11.2	9.3	8.8	7.7
Domestic demand	8.8	7.6	5.3	6.0	5.8	5.5	5.8	5.9
Real retail sales	10.0	10.2	8.0	8.5	7.0	7.0	8.2	8.0
Real wages	18.0	22.0	12.5	12.0	8.0	5.7	6.8	5.8
Rouble year-end ($)	28.2	30.5	31.9	30.2	31.9	33.9	36.0	37.5

Note: 2000–02 figures are actual; 2003–07 figures are estimates.
Source: Nenad Pacek and Daniel Thorniley

a financial bubble by issuing government treasury bills with huge yields of 70–100%, reserves are strong and the central bank has learnt some hard lessons about currency management. There is also scope for the currency to fall.

The effect of oil price changes
If the oil price collapses in the near future, the Russian economy and eventually western companies will be hit. This must be factored into business plans. The Russian economy is still overly dependent on oil, gas and other commodities, and more than 50% of export revenue still comes from energy and oil products. But there is room for cautious optimism. The oil price is likely to stay around $23–25 per barrel for a couple of years before falling to around $18–20. Russia makes a tiny profit on oil at $14 per barrel, a reasonable profit at $17 per barrel and things are rosy at over $20 per barrel.

However, it can be argued that at best Russia has two years to introduce more fundamental structural reforms to get its economy going at higher levels of growth and to get away gradually from its energy dependence. How long this window of opportunity endures after the 2004 presidential elections will depend mostly on the oil price. But the direction and speed of structural reforms in 2004–07 will be a decisive factor in forging Russia's economic future for the next 10–20 years. Starts on restructuring have been made but are moving slowly. The risk is that reforms do not kick in in time and that GDP trends remain below potential for too long.

Russia will join the WTO

The government's stated aim is to join the World Trade Organisation (WTO) as soon as possible. Proper negotiations are likely to start after the 2004 presidential elections. Entry in 2006 or 2007 is possible, which would help improve the perception of the Russian market among foreign investors and might bring the medium-term benefits to business and investment that China experienced on its accession. But there is a long way to go. On balance, it is likely to be later rather than sooner.

Many Russian industrial companies are against WTO entry, at least before 2007. Sectors that would come under pressure and offer western companies opportunities include aerospace, furniture and timber, financial services, telecommunications, agriculture and automotives. They all have strong lobbies with good connections to President Putin; the automotive sector, for example, managed to get import duties raised in 2002.

Western executives should benchmark the impact of WTO entry on China over the next few years and weigh the pros and cons over the medium term. Managers in the telecoms sector have warned their colleagues in other sectors to start reading the draft documents that are likely to be presented to the Russian authorities. Overall, WTO changes are beneficial to western investors, but the fine print in some clauses may include details that could harm current business strategies or at least make them more complicated or expensive.

Receivables: not too many bad debts

The notion that it is difficult to get paid in Russia is wrong. In a 2003 survey of 100 western companies doing business in Russia conducted by The Economist Corporate Network in Vienna, 75% of respondents thought the situation with receivables would remain acceptable to good, 23% felt there would be improvements and only 5% thought there would be any worsening.

In 2002 the average number of days to collect receivables in Russia was 45, which compares favourably with other emerging markets. Payment terms were lengthening in 2003, and this trend should continue as competition picks up and companies have to offer more favourable terms. An increasing number of western pharmaceuticals and consumer goods companies are offering 90–120 days as they do in the West, and few complain of non-payment. One large American engineering company says: "We have been doing business in Russia for 20 years and never lost a dollar in payments." Russia is a paper-driven society. If you have the right papers, you will win in court; if you do not, regardless of the spirit of the law, you will not.

Tax: huge improvements have been made

Any notion that tax is the death of western business in Russia is wrong. Some 95% of western managers, all law firms and the big four accountancy firms agree that there have been huge improvements in taxation in Russia in the past few years. The introduction of a much lower rate of personal tax (13%, compared with a range rising to 35%) appears not to have dented tax receipts. Corporate tax has come down to 24% from 35%. A radical overhaul of the tax penalty system has been implemented and tax inspectors can no longer harass western companies and get away with it. In the courts, the burden of proof in tax cases is in favour of the western company. The main change in the tax environment, however, is the ability to deduct all necessary and evident business expenses, including advertising, training, recruitment, legal, consulting and auditing.

Intellectual property: mixed at best

The laws on intellectual property look good on paper, but implementation leaves something to be desired. Microsoft has had some successes as have brand names such as Reebok, but infringements in the pharmaceuticals sector have been getting worse. The Russian civil and criminal authorities are now working together better, which is one key to success. Most importantly, Russia's desire to join the WTO provides an incentive to get on top of intellectual property issues.

The legal environment

Russia is not the "Wild East". Western law firms report that they are winning 90% of their cases in Russia compared with 50% in the West. Western companies of any size can win, and the cost is lower than in the West. An average commercial case takes 3–5 months.

Another positive trend is that, in general, laws are now not just Yeltsin-era decrees but are federal in nature and enacted by the Duma, so they have more chance of being properly implemented. But some western industrial companies complain that there can be a lack of consistency, especially outside the big cities. As one American manager complained: "They simply haven't heard what the new laws are."

In the past, companies generally set up a representative office in Russia. Now they are increasingly forming legal entities and subsidiaries. This is encouraging the "Russification of business and law", with structures and litigation referring more to Russian law and courts. Western companies are becoming increasingly comfortable with this. Indeed, on issues of arbitration, western law firms advise their clients to choose Moscow as a location rather than Stockholm or Geneva as it simplifies the process and there is just as much chance of a positive result. Attaching assets after a successful arbitration can be as difficult as it is anywhere else. Often, though, the threat of a court case frightens companies into settling.

When a western company loses a case in a remote region, it can often appeal in a regional centre and win, and as the case gets closer to Moscow, its chances of winning increase. The western media often report an initial ruling which has gone against a western investor but fail to note the successful appeal several months later. Hence the often negative perception of the Russian commercial legal system.

Nothing is perfect, however, and lawyers advise caution when taking organisations with powerful Russian vested interests to court. It may not be so simple to get a favourable ruling in the Moscow courts against an organisation that has the support of, say, the mayor of Moscow.

You can trust your Russian business partner – most of the time

"Our Russian distributors are more trustworthy than our German ones," says the regional manager of a large American IT company. The Russian commercial environment is built on personal relationships, trust and partnerships, and commercial judgments are often based on instinct. This is not always easy to incorporate into a company's business processes. Time, effort and consideration are needed to build relationships with distributors or joint-venture partners to get good returns. This can take a lot of energy, but if western companies and investors want to build solid commercial relations, this is part of the deal.

Following the rouble crash in August 1998, it was commonly assumed that Russian companies fleeced their western partners. Some Russian distributors pretended to go bust and did not pay their bills, but just as many did go bust and could not pay their bills. What is less well known is that many Russian partners went the extra mile to pay their western suppliers in the months following the crisis. Dozens of western pharmaceuticals, consumer goods and manufacturing companies reported that their distributors were paying them via bank accounts in Liechtenstein, Vienna and London.

Managers at a German automotive company found themselves with a $21m exposure to a new Russian business partner when the rouble crashed. They thought their careers were over as they went to their ultra-conservative German board to tell them of the loss. But then the Russian company deposited the $21m in the German company's bank account in Moscow.

Of course western companies do get ripped off in Russia, just as they do anywhere in the world. One consumer goods company operating in St Petersburg says that it has lost a couple of shipments each worth $100,000 in recent years. But it also says that this is not something that only happens in Russia.

One manager supports the general view that partners and distributors in Russia are trustworthy but elaborated as follows:

> *They are generally very honest partners and individual relationships work well. But it is when you get beyond personal contacts that you find there is more graft and corruption within institutions. It is nothing outrageous for an emerging market but institutional graft does exist.*

Western lawyers speaking in 2003 seem to share this view: "There is some bribery in Russia but really nothing above the norm of emerging markets."

Personal safety
Moscow is as safe as most cities in Europe. Of course it has "no-go areas", and sensible caution is required. Muggings and even some car-jackings do take place, but again nothing more than in London or Amsterdam. Often the biggest danger to personal safety is the potholes in the street.

Satisfying staff
The Soviet system got many things wrong, but its education system was one of its stronger points. A regional manager of a large IT company says:

> *Our staff in Russia are the best in the world: better than in central Europe, better than in western Europe, and better than in the United States.*

Western companies report huge satisfaction with their Russian staff at all levels. They are not always the best sales or marketing people, but with the right training they can be. The Soviet education system ensured that students were trained, often by rote, in a structured, disciplined manner so that they mastered chemistry, physics, maths, biology and engineering. They were not as good at social studies and history, but their brains had been trained to work. Western companies find this a great resource to work on.

One of the tragedies in Russia in the last 12 years is that investment in the education system has plummeted. It has not yet affected the quality of Russian human resources, largely because of the quality and dedication of the poorly paid Russian teaching staff. Also at the margins, local business schools are starting up and high-quality Russian students are winning more scholarships abroad. These then often develop into talented staff on the books of western companies.

The poaching of good staff is increasing; many Russian employees are looking for large pay packets or more non-financial inducements and benefits. Many larger Russian companies are contributing to wage inflation by offering the best Russian staff salaries that are 25–100% higher than market rates. As the market for staff in Moscow and St Petersburg tightens, more investors enter the market and the pool of qualified Russians remains static, a growing number of companies are experiencing staffing problems.

The best Russian staff are perceived to be people who were in their early 20s in 1991. They were well educated under the Soviet system, are not "contaminated" by Soviet ideology and experience, are more open to new ideas and training than their older peers, and are willing to work hard for moderate salaries. Their elders were thought (in many cases unfairly) not to be adaptable. The problem now is that the Russian educational system is suffering from underinvestment. New graduates are less well educated and less conscientious than older people and are "contaminated" by the capitalist system, in the sense that they want to "get rich quick". This is, of course, a sweeping generalisation, but there is some truth in it. Perhaps those now in their early 30s are the "golden generation" from an employment point of view.

What's not so good about doing business in Russia?

Based on the above figures and anecdotes, a lot is going well, but few executives are naively optimistic. The drawbacks of the economy and business environment include the following.

- Domestic investment is volatile.
- The oil price risk. There is still dependence on oil and commodity prices. When oil is under $20 per barrel, pressures on the Russian economy increase.
- Diversification into non-energy manufactures is still slow.
- Corporate governance. There is some improvement among larger Russian companies but still a long way to go.
- The potential for GDP growth is substantial – and it should be borne in mind that Russia will not catch up with Portuguese GDP per head over the next ten years unless it can achieve 5–6% annual growth over that period.
- Foreign direct investment remains low.
- The banking sector is immature, inefficient and lacks probity. It will take as many as ten years to get it into a shape considered acceptable by western standards. Russian banks provide only 6% of the financing resources required by Russian enterprises, which obtain the remainder of their financing predominantly from reinvested profits, returning capital flight or limited western partnerships. Western banks are not particularly interested in investing in the market, although Citibank has dipped into the local retail market, where Austrian banks have taken the lead.
- Russia is still an expensive place to do business. It takes an inordinate amount of managerial time and energy because regional executives have to spend so much time (and thus money) challenging and overcoming the prejudices of senior managers at headquarters.
- There is room for improvement in corporate and legislative transparency. Rules on corporate governance are not as developed as in the West and legislation may be difficult to interpret or implement.
- Minority shareholder rights remain inadequate.
- Crime and corruption remain issues of concern, even though the "Wild East" is not as wild as sometimes portrayed.
- The customs regime has severe operational difficulties. It started to improve in 2001 and a new customs law in 2004 should help further.
- Capital flight is still a problem.
- Some sectors, such as food, beverages, consumer goods, consumer durables and IT, have been better for western companies than others, such as agriculture and construction.

◪ There has not been enough restructuring in the economy and there has been too much focus on the oil price.

Why is foreign direct investment so weak?

Total foreign direct investment (FDI) in Russia since 1991 is only $35 billion, equivalent to less than one year's investment in China. Is Russia really that bad? Paul Melling is a senior partner at Baker & McKenzie, a global law firm, and one of the most experienced western lawyers working in Moscow. He says:

> I just don't understand why foreign investment is so low. What is keeping investors out? Three or four years ago, yes, there were several problems and valid reasons. But now nearly all of these have disappeared, particularly those with a tax and legal perspective. More FDI should be coming in, but it is not.

Being a good lawyer he came up with several reasons.

◪ Western companies have strong memories of the 1998 crash when some were taken to the cleaners by Russian partners or heard stories of such events. Some Russian companies left bankrupt shells. Corporate governance has improved among the larger Russian companies but there is still a long way to go.
◪ The Russians themselves have a love-hate relationship with all things western and this applies to western business and western investors. They want all the benefits of FDI but are unwilling to work for this.
◪ Only a handful of Russian regions make outside investors welcome, including Moscow, Moscow region, St Petersburg, Novgorod and Nizhnii Novgorod. The other 84 regions are either indifferent or do not have the experience to work professionally with outsiders.
◪ There are virtually no tax incentives. Russia must understand that it has to compete in the global economy to attract inward investment.
◪ The government and Putin should employ a good PR agency. The message about Russia is simply not getting across. All the good news is swamped in the negative portrayal of the country, which is largely unfair and inaccurate.
◪ The authorities would be well advised to revamp Sheremetyevo,

the main Moscow airport. All the prejudices of senior managers (and tourists) are reinforced when they see the sleaze and gloom pervading the airport complex. Thankfully, this is mitigated by the bright lights and consumerism on Tverskaya ulitsa, the main thoroughfare in downtown Moscow.

There seems to be an "emotional barrier" in convincing headquarters of the benefits of a Russian investment strategy. One executive underlined the risks:

You want to avoid looking like an idiot or a manic risk-taker.
Those who want to sabotage your plans will always find a
case and be able to question your financial assumptions.

The debate on Russia often takes place against a background of office power play among managers who want to invest in other regions of the world or not at all. Russia takes up a huge amount of managerial time and energy because the internal corporate debate is so demanding.

But the tide may be turning. With EU accession completed for the core central and eastern European countries in 2004 and the major south-east European ones in 2007–08, the big player in terms of a market with less competition, greater growth opportunities and lower wage costs is Russia. The announcements by BP and Shell of large investments in the Russian energy sector will help adjust preconceptions. Given the number of companies now taking a fresh look at Russia, investment could soon increase significantly. There is almost always a time lag between the realisation that the investment climate in a market has changed and the decision to invest, and another before the decision translates into improved statistics.

Statistics on corporate location decisions in 2002, collected by the IBM Global Investment Location Database, show a sharper focus on Russia. It took 5% of the global cake compared with 4% for Mexico, 4.5% for Brazil and 13% for China. In the food and drinks sector, Russia was the number one location, taking a 14% share of announced global investment projects. It came third in plastics and rubber investments with a 7% share, second in metals with 6%, third in electronics with 6% and fifth in life sciences with 5%. The Economist Intelligence Unit estimates that annual FDI into Russia will jump from an annual average of $2–3 billion in 1995–2002 to $9 billion in 2003 and remain at this level for several years. Russia would then soon surpass other central Europe locations, as well as many in Latin America and South-East Asia, in terms of accumulated FDI.

Other CIS markets

As stated in Chapter 15, as a general benchmark for the majority of companies, the "85–10–5" rule applies to doing business in the former Soviet Union. This means that in most business sectors 85% of a company's business is carried out in Russia, 10% in Ukraine and 5% in the other republics. This of course excludes energy and commodity companies.

Caucasus

Overall, there are few business opportunities in the Caucasus, a large region between the Black Sea and the Caspian Sea that includes Armenia, Azerbaijan and Georgia. The market is poor and the risks are high. Companies that do business in the region invariably do so opportunistically via distributors with pre-payment.

Central Asian republics

The same applies to the Central Asian republics, where corruption is just as rampant as in the Caucasus. Many of them are becoming family-run fiefdoms. In the 1990s, some general manufacturing companies tried to set up manufacturing operations in the region, as did some food companies, but all ended in failure. Large services companies that tried to enter the market were blocked by corruption, and opposition came from within the Kazakhstan leadership. Banks and health companies that set up operations or representative offices have been generally disappointed, and currency conversion is a major headache.

Some western companies have reported sales growth of up to 50% but from fairly small bases. Again, most business is conducted at low risk with pre-payment the norm. Overall, the business outlook for the next five years is bleak for western companies that wish to conduct regular business on regular terms.

Belarus

Belarus, where Alexander Lukashenko continues to run one of the last Soviet-style economies in the world, remains another isolated island for western business. Suppressed inflation of the Soviet kind is the only thing preventing a total economic collapse with severe social and economic consequences. There is no likelihood of any real rapprochement with Russia until the regime changes.

Ukraine

Business is picking up in Ukraine. Only a few years ago, less than 5% of western companies – including some consumer goods, beer and tobacco companies, a bank and an automotive company – were satisfied with their sales. Since 2000, however, the figure has risen to about 40%. A number of companies are reporting stronger growth in Ukraine than in Russia. These include some health care companies, which in 2002 reported sales increases of as much as 50% in Ukraine compared with 30% in Russia; some services and consumer goods companies have noted the same trend.

The improvement occurred because Ukraine finally bounced back – a little more slowly than Russia – from the rouble collapse which damaged its economy. Viktor Yushchenko's government brought some temporary stability and there were reforms in economic policy. The currency stabilised and inflation came down. Real wages rose in 2000 for only the second time in nine years of independence, and they rose again in 2001 and 2002.

Improving sales have encouraged consumer goods companies to consider upgrading their local presence to legal entity status and to reassess how they manage their Ukraine operations. They are increasingly likely to operate hands-on in Ukraine, rather than managing everything from Moscow, although they will have to decide to which office the Ukraine operations should report: directly to European headquarters or to an expanding Moscow office, which will handle the CIS business and perhaps develop an independent shared services set-up within the company. Opinions within companies vary on which option is best.

Few companies are satisfied with the commercial environment, complaining about bureaucracy, red tape, insider deals, corruption, ineffectual laws, poor administration and so on. Furthermore, Ukraine has done little over the years to improve things. Indeed, several managers believe that the level of corruption increased in 2002 from already high levels. One manager of a pharmaceuticals company said: "I feel comfortable with a Russian contract. But a contract in Ukraine just isn't worth anything." Another western manager complained:

> *The mafias just don't get it: they take everything for themselves and leave nothing for Ukrainian and western businessmen. If they had sense they would leave us something so we could carry on. They're just not sophisticated and too greedy. They kill the golden goose.*

Is the pick-up in business sustainable? The risks in Ukraine are much higher than in Russia. The country is not resource-rich and does not have significant oil reserves; political uncertainty is worrying and the alliances between political parties remain fragile; political gridlock has a negative effect on reform legislation; and privatisations are thwarted because too small a share is offered for too high a price.

If things go well, in five years or so Ukraine, along with Russia, could represent a major growth market for western investors. Some were considering entering the agro-food sector a couple of years ago as business picked up, but they were put off by a political scandal involving President Kuchma and the murder of a journalist.

Meanwhile, Russians have been buying up assets in energy, oil, transport, beer, agro-food, metals and other export sectors. When western investors pluck up the courage to invest, they often find themselves catching the plane to Moscow to conduct negotiations. And the Russians won't be selling cheaply.

Appendix 1 Comparative tables

Table A1 **Central and eastern Europe: market size, 2003**[a]

	GDP (US$bn)	Imports (US$bn)	Population (m)
Albania	6.2	1.8	3.1
Armenia	2.4	1.0	3.0
Azerbaijan	5.9	2.2	8.3
Belarus	14.0	8.8	10.0
Bosnia & Hercegovina	5.6	4.5	4.0
Bulgaria	12.0	10.0	7.8
Croatia	25.4	13.1	4.5
Cyprus	11.5	4.5	0.7
Czech Republic	63.4	48.6	10.3
Estonia	6.2	5.6	1.4
Georgia	4.0	1.3	4.4
Hungary	59.8	45.6	10.1
Kazakhstan	32.0	7.9	14.8
Kyrgyz Republic	2.0	0.6	5.1
Latvia	7.7	4.7	2.3
Lithuania	11.3	9.4	3.5
Macedonia	5.0	2.3	2.1
Malta	4.6	2.8	0.4
Moldova	1.9	1.3	3.6
Poland	184.5	64.3	38.2
Romania	36.9	23.0	21.7
Russia	511.5	74.7	144.9
Serbia & Montenegro	14.9	7.5	10.7
Slovakia	26.2	22.3	5.4
Slovenia	24.5	12.7	2.0
Tajikistan	1.2	0.8	6.4
Turkey	214.6	67.0	71.3
Turkmenistan	9.0	2.6	4.7
Ukraine	54.6	21.8	48.0
Uzbekistan	18.1	2.3	25.8
Total[b]	1,376.7	439.0	478.1

a Figures are estimates.　b Figures may not add because of rounding.

Table A2 **Western Europe: market size, 2003[a]**

	GDP (US$bn)	Imports (US$bn)	Population (m)
Austria	260.4	83.0	8.2
Belgium	303.1	213.2	10.3
Denmark	212.6	54.3	5.4
Finland	158.6	45.8	5.2
France	1,809.0	347.0	60.2
Germany	2,552.5	582.0	82.5
Greece	145.0	38.5	10.6
Iceland	9.3	2.7	0.3
Ireland	126.8	58.4	3.9
Italy	1,393.2	289.8	58.2
Luxembourg	25.0	13.2	0.5
Netherlands	471.6	212.3	16.2
Norway	186.6	38.4	4.5
Portugal	129.4	41.6	10.3
Spain	744.7	202.3	40.8
Sweden	328.0	85.7	9.0
Switzerland	324.7	84.1	7.3
UK	1,432.9	356.9	60.3
Total[b]	10,613.3	2,749.3	393.7

a Figures are estimates.   b Figures may not add because of rounding.

Table A3 **North America: market size, 2003[a]**

	GDP (US$bn)	Imports (US$bn)	Population (m)
Canada	792.7	242.8	31.7
US	9,721.1	1,241.7	289.5
Total[b]	10,513.8	1,484.5	321.2

a Figures are estimates.   b Figures may not add because of rounding.

Table A4 **South America: market size, 2003[a]**

	GDP (US$bn)	Imports (US$bn)	Population (m)
Argentina	268.6	14.9	38.2
Aruba	1.8	2.0	0.1
Bahamas	5.2	1.8	0.3
Barbados	n/a	1.0	0.3
Belize	n/a	0.5	0.3
Bermuda	3.7	0.1	0.1
Bolivia	9.0	1.8	9.0
Brazil	872.7	49.6	177.5
Caribbean	n/a	n/a	n/a
Cayman Islands	n/a	n/a	n/a
Chile	93.6	18.5	15.2
Colombia	105.5	13.4	44.6
Costa Rica	16.1	7.5	4.2
Cuba	25.4	4.3	11.3
Dominican Republic	18.5	5.1	8.9
Ecuador	24.2	6.0	12.6
El Salvador	12.4	5.8	6.5
Guatemala	19.9	6.2	12.4
Guyana	n/a	0.6	0.8
Haiti	3.0	1.0	8.3
Honduras	4.9	3.2	7.0
Jamaica	6.6	3.7	2.6
Mexico	420.7	168.3	103.3
Netherlands Antilles	2.4	1.5	0.2
Nicaragua	2.5	1.8	5.5
Panama	11.0	3.2	3.1
Paraguay	10.0	1.5	5.9
Peru	67.8	8.2	27.2
Puerto Rico	n/a	29.0	3.9
Suriname	n/a	0.3	0.4
Trinidad & Tobago	8.0	4.1	1.3
Turks & Caicos Islands	0.2	0.2	0.02
Uruguay	18.4	2.3	3.4
Venezuela	59.5	11.3	24.7
Virgin Islands	0.8	0.2	0.02
Total[b]	2,092.3	372.0	539.0

a Figures are estimates.   b Figures may not add because of rounding.

Table A5 Asia: market size, 2003[a]

	GDP (US$bn)	Imports (US$bn)	Population (m)
Afghanistan	4.0	2.3	26.0
Australia	517.7	82.9	19.8
Bangladesh	58.1	8.9	146.8
Bhutan	0.6	n/a	0.7
Brunei	n/a	n/a	0.4
Cambodia	3.9	2.1	14.2
China	1,390.1	402.1	1,295.2
East Timor	0.4	0.2	n/a
Fiji	n/a	0.6	0.8
Hong Kong	186.6	230.2	6.9
India	554.8	66.8	1,061.6
Indonesia	243.2	32.5	216.2
Japan	5,030.7	395.4	127.0
Laos	2.1	0.5	5.7
Macau	n/a	2.5	0.4
Malaysia	125.6	84.7	25.0
Mongolia	1.1	0.7	2.6
Myanmar	8.2	2.5	49.6
Nepal	n/a	0.9	23.7
New Caledonia	n/a	1.1	0.3
New Zealand	80.9	16.7	4.0
North Korea	n/a	1.9	22.4
Pakistan	78.1	13.6	150.7
Papua New Guinea	4.8	1.1	5.7
Philippines	105.9	39.4	84.6
Samoa	n/a	0.1	0.2
Singapore	114.6	127.1	4.2
Solomon Islands	n/a	n/a	0.5
South Korea	696.0	173.3	48.2
Sri Lanka	18.5	6.8	19.1
Taiwan	363.9	123.3	22.6
Thailand	199.5	71.7	64.0
Tonga	n/a	n/a	0.1
Vanuatu	n/a	n/a	0.2
Vietnam	38.7	23.0	81.4
Total[b]	9,827.8	1,901.6	3,530.7

a Figures are estimates.   b Figures may not add because of rounding.

Table A6 **Middle East and North Africa: market size, 2003[a]**

	GDP (US$bn)	Imports (US$bn)	Population (m)
Algeria	60.1	13.2	31.3
Bahrain	8.4	5.6	0.7
Egypt	90.4	15.1	71.9
Iran	115.1	23.7	69.3
Iraq	17.2	7.9	25.2
Israel	115.9	32.9	6.7
Jordan	8.9	5.7	5.5
Kuwait	33.5	9.4	2.5
Lebanon	13.9	6.6	3.7
Libya	30.7	4.4	5.6
Morocco	44.9	13.5	30.6
Saudi Arabia	185.3	33.9	24.3
Syria	18.9	5.6	17.8
Tunisia	27.2	10.7	9.8
United Arab Emirates	66.2	40.7	4.0
Yemen	7.5	3.5	20.0
Total[b]	844.1	232.4	328.7

a Figures are estimates.   b Figures may not add because of rounding.

Table A7 **Sub-saharan Africa: market size, 2003[a]**

	GDP (US$bn)	Imports (US$bn)	Population (m)
Angola	8.9	4.9	14.3
Benin	2.8	0.7	6.7
Botswana	8.0	2.0	1.8
Burkina Faso	2.8	0.4	12.8
Burundi	0.6	0.1	6.9
Cameroon	12.4	2.0	16.2
Cape Verde	0.6	0.3	0.5
Central African Republic	1.0	0.1	3.9
Chad	1.9	0.8	8.6
Comoros	0.1	0.1	0.8
Congo (Brazzaville)	2.2	0.7	3.3
Congo (Democratic Republic)	5.6	1.4	54.6
Côte d'Ivoire	12.9	2.9	16.6
Djibouti	0.7	0.3	0.7

	GDP (US$bn)	Imports (US$bn)	Population (m)
Equatorial Guinea	2.4	0.8	0.5
Eritrea	0.5	0.5	4.0
Ethiopia	6.0	1.7	66.2
Gabon	6.2	1.1	1.3
Gambia	0.2	0.2	1.5
Ghana	9.3	3.5	20.9
Guinea	3.2	0.7	8.4
Guinea-Bissau	0.1	0.1	1.3
Kenya	10.1	3.3	32.0
Lesotho	0.7	0.7	2.3
Liberia	0.4	0.2	2.9
Madagascar	5.0	0.7	16.9
Malawi	2.8	0.6	12.1
Mali	3.2	0.6	12.0
Mauritania	1.0	0.4	2.9
Mauritius	6.1	2.5	1.2
Mozambique	4.1	−1.3	18.5
Namibia	4.3	1.5	2.0
Niger	1.9	0.4	11.6
Nigeria	42.6	14.3	133.2
Oman	19.8	6.2	2.6
Qatar	17.3	4.4	0.6
Rwanda	1.9	0.3	8.3
São Tomé & Príncipe	0.1	0.03	0.1
Senegal	6.4	2.0	10.3
Seychelles	0.5	0.4	0.1
Sierra Leone	0.8	0.2	4.9
Somalia	n/a	n/a	10.9
South Africa	169.5	30.7	45.7
Sudan	12.4	2.6	33.6
Swaziland	1.2	1.1	1.1
Tanzania	9.0	1.6	36.2
Togo	1.4	0.8	4.8
Uganda	8.3	1.6	26.5
Zambia	3.9	1.1	10.8
Zimbabwe	5.9	1.7	13.1
Total[b]	428.7	103.0	709.0

a Figures are estimates.   b Figures may not add because of rounding.

Table A8 **Foreign direct investment inflows in developing countries, 1985–2006 ($bn)**

1985	13.3
1986	12.9
1987	12.8
1988	22.4
1989	26.9
1990	33.8
1991	44.2
1992	56.7
1993	79.6
1994	111.0
1995	127.5
1996	162.2
1997	208.7
1998	213.5
1999	237.7
2000	259.8
2001	237.2
2002	234.9
2003	266.8
2004	286.8
2005	304.3
2006	329.5

Note: Figures for 1985–2002 are actual; figures for 2003–06 are estimates.

Table A9 **Foreign direct investment inflows in selected regions, 1991–2006 ($bn)**

	Developing Asia	China	Latin America & the Caribbean	Transition economies	Middle East	Sub-saharan Africa
1991	21.1	4.4	15.6	n/a	1.8	2.1
1992	27.9	11.2	18.3	n/a	2.5	1.6
1993	47.8	27.5	16.7	7.5	3.8	1.9
1994	64.9	33.8	30.5	7.4	2.2	3.5
1995	72.6	35.8	32.4	16.5	1.2	4.2
1996	86.6	40.2	49.8	15.8	4.8	4.5
1997	96.7	44.2	73.7	22.3	7.0	8.2
1998	87.0	43.8	85.1	25.4	8.0	6.1
1999	92.6	38.8	105.2	27.8	3.7	7.0
2000	132.0	38.4	89.0	27.8	4.7	5.7
2001	99.6	46.8	83.0	28.2	7.9	13.1
2002	110.0	50.0	68.5	33.6	9.5	9.2
2003	121.1	55.0	80.5	33.7	14.5	11.0
2004	130.2	60.0	85.3	34.8	15.6	12.5
2005	138.8	65.0	90.1	36.6	16.3	13.1
2006	150.5	72.0	96.8	38.9	18.1	13.9

Note: Figures for 1991–2002 are actual; figures for 2003–06 are estimates.

Source for all tables: The Economist Intelligence Unit

Appendix 2 **References**

The authors have used the following sources.

PART 1
General
The Economist
The *Financial Times*

6 Interpreting economic indicators
The Economist Guide to Economic Indicators, 5th edition, Profile Books, 2003.

10 Making acquisitions work

Bibler, R.S., *The Arthur Young Management Guide to Mergers and Acquisitions*, John Wiley and Sons, 1989.
The Economist Intelligence Unit, *Foreign Investment in Eastern Europe*, 1993.
Rock, M.L., Rock, R.H. and Sikora, M., *The Mergers and Acquisitions Handbook*, 2nd edition, McGraw-Hill, 1994.

14 Understanding and coping with emerging-market crises

Krugman, P., *The Return of Depression Economics*, Allen Lane, Penguin Books, 1999.
Stiglitz, J.E., *Globalization and its Discontents*, Allen Lane, The Penguin Press, 2002.

PART 2
Reports
The Economist
The Economist Intelligence Unit
The *Financial Times*
The *Guardian*
The *Independent*
The IMF
The *Observer*
The OECD
The World Bank

Research reports

Commerzbank
Credit Suisse First Boston
Deutsche Bank

Index